Praise for *The Creator Mindset*

"Bashan is one of our smartest thinkers out there today at the intersection of work, creativity, and society."

—**Michael Morsberger**, Vice President of
Advancement at University of Central Florida,
and CEO of the UCF Foundation

"I'd long assumed that creativity is a rare gift that only a handful of lucky people are born with. Boy was I wrong! As Nir will show you, creativity is a tool anyone can learn, deploy, and benefit from. In a commoditized world where businesses blindly rely on analytics to determine potential outcomes, the value of The Creator Mindset—and rethinking traditional ways of doing things—has never been greater. Great rewards await those willing to shake things up. Unleash The Creator Mindset before your competitors do! It's easier than you think!"

—**Ken Schmidt**, author of *Make Some Noise* and
former Director of Communications at
Harley-Davidson Motor Company

"Nir Bashan is the first author I know to write about creativity and to lead the reader through a truly effective way of developing it. As a leader, I always encouraged my teammates to be creative but didn't really know what I was asking. Now I do. This book helps us all do more than encourage creativity—it puts us in the position of knowing what that means and how to help our people get there. My grasp of creativity and how to leverage it has more than doubled after reading this book. I'm a much better leader as a result. In times when so many businesses and organizations have to adapt, creativity is the coin of the realm. Nir Bashan has banked it for us in this book."

—Brig. Gen Thomas Kolditz, PhD,
Director of Rice University's Doerr Institute
for New Leaders

"From business schools to boardrooms, the prevailing wisdom is that value is generated through efficiency and productivity. Both are quantifiable; they show up on a spreadsheet. Bashan encourages us to think beyond the spreadsheet. He makes the case for value generation through creativity, and then provides a step-by-step guide for anyone to unleash it."

—Jae Goodman, CEO of Observatory (a Stagwell
and CAA Company), four-time Emmy and Cannes
Lions Grand Prix winner, and one of Fast Company's
"World's Most Innovative Companies"

"Nir Bashan's The Creator Mindset is one of the first books I have read that takes people who believe they have little, or no creativity, and guides them through the ups and downs of becoming creative. This book will be shared rapidly throughout companies and organizations."

—Anthony Reeves, global creative leader,
keynote speaker, and business change consultant

"Bashan argues passionately in *The Creator Mindset* about creativity being something we are all born with. And he has made a convert of me. This is one book you do not want to miss this year."
—**Dr. John Whyte**, MD, MPH,
Chief Medical Officer at WebMD

"Nir Bashan has written an inspiring book on the importance of creativity in all aspects of life and business, one filled with helpful exercises on how to be an innovative thinker. It will make the world a more creative place."
—**AJ Jacobs**, author of *Thanks a Thousand*

"A timely provocation with easily applicable tools to enable people—particularly those who don't consider themselves 'creative'—to put new ideas in the world. Yes, thank you, more please."
—**Marcus Collins**, lecturer of Marketing and
Co-Director of the Yaffe Digital Media Initiative
Ross School of Business at University of Michigan

"Here's an inspiring and informed how-to guide for tapping into a largely overlooked tool for innovation—ourselves! Nir Bashan seamlessly weaves historical accounts of the rise of titans of business with charming tales of his childhood entrepreneurial endeavors to complement the concrete and effective techniques he offers for ingeniously unlocking our own creative potential."
—**Emily Balcetis**, author of *Clearer, Closer, Better*
and Associate Professor of Psychology at
New York University

"*The Creator Mindset* contains research, storytelling, and humor that guides the reader to thinking creatively in all they do."
—**Mark C. Thompson**, bestselling author, Venture
Investor and Founder Stanford University Realtime
Venture Design Lab, and Board of Directors for Smule

"*The Creator Mindset* will inspire you to act! Bashan makes a strong case for the importance of creativity in every business and the potential to unlock the creative side in every person. He provides tools that are easy to follow and allow you to develop The Creator Mindset in yourself."

—**Kerstin Emhoff**, CEO of Prettybird / Ventureland

"Fun and delightful! Creativity is essential for success in geopolitics as well as business, and *The Creator Mindset* reminds us how to tap and unleash the natural creativity we all possess."

—**Douglas P. Wickert**, Colonel, USAF, Permanent Professor, and Head of the Department of Aeronautics at US Air Force Academy

"I loved how *The Creator Mindset* gave me a concrete framework to approach business challenges with the same ingenuity that I used throughout military career. *The Creator Mindset* will teach you with the same 'adapt and overcome' mentality that I developed during my years flying in an F/A-18 flying at Mach 1, just with less studying and more relatable stories!"

—**Caroline Johnson**, author of *JetGirl*

"In *The Creator Mindset*, Nir Bashan compellingly and charmingly argues that creativity is more than afterthought in business—it's the centerpiece of any successful venture, and even entrepreneurs who don't consider themselves creative naturals can master the science and art of creativity by adopting Bashan's Creator Mindset. An important, convincing, and enjoyable book that should be required reading for entrepreneurs everywhere."

—**Adam Alter**, Professor of Marketing and Psychology at New York University and *New York Times* bestselling author of *Irresistible* and *Drunk Tank Pink*

"This delightful book explains how anyone in business can adopt The Creator Mindset, helping themselves and their companies to thrive. Emphasizing character, listening, and using mistakes to learn fast, Nir Bashan offers timeless insights in an approachable, engaging style." •

> —**Amy C. Edmondson,** Professor of Leadership and Management at Harvard Business Schcool and author of *The Fearless Organization*

"An action-oriented guide for unlocking creativity. Nir's argument, that all of us must become more creative is forceful and convincing. But more importantly, he explains how organizations and individual creators can rise to the occasion."

> —**Allen Gannett,** author of *The Creative Curve*

"Better than the classic *Who Moved My Cheese?*, *The Creator Mindset* brings creativity in business to life through storytelling at its best."

> —**Lorraine Justice,** PhD, author of *The Future of Design*

"Creativity is something we all have, now there is finally a book that can help you harness this 'superpower.' For far too long a myth has been perpetuated that creativity is limited to a special few. Nir busts this myth wide open. His book presents a clear and well-researched step-by-step approach that allows you to tap into your Creator Mindset."

> —**Richard Turrin,** author of *Innovation Lab Excellence* and former head of IBM Cognitive Studios Singapore

"Love this book. Easy to read. Informative with some simple pragmatic steps which will help boost creativity. Everyone should read this book!"

> —**Gordon Tredgold,** Global Gurus Top 10 Leadership expert and speaker

"A creative mind sees what can be rather than what is. In a world of crises and opportunities, the ability to see what can be is priceless. Yet, many of us invest heavily in developing our analytical minds, but underinvest in our creative minds. Nir's path to a Creator Mindset restores the balance. That's probably never been more important than now."

—**Ajay Agrawal**, University of Toronto professor,
founder of the Creative Destruction Lab, and author
of *Prediction Machines*

"Guys like Nir can read the zeitgeist and share amazing insights that are actionable and interesting. Read this book as soon as you can."

—**John Biggs**, writer, entrepreneur, and bestselling author

"Nir Bashan teaches us how to cultivate our creativity by learning and living The Creator Mindset. Written in an engaging, readable style, this book is filled with memorable examples, vivid stories, and practical tools that will inspire you and enable you to unleash your creativity and fulfill your potential."

—**Wayne Baker**, The Robert P. Thome Professor of
Business Administration and Faculty Director of the
Center for Positive Organizations at the University
of Michigan Ross School of Business and author of
All You Have to Do Is Ask

"This book is a firm reminder that being creative isn't just for artists; we use creativity to give us a competitive edge in all parts of life, whether it be in business or sports. Finding that success means recognizing that we aren't machines; we are a species BUILD machines and solve problems in unique ways. *The Creator Mindset* is a guide to maximize your creativity for moments in life that require fundamental change, all with the ultimate goal of living a stronger and happier life."

—**J.F. Musial**, President & CEO of TangentVector

"It has been said that management is 'doing things right' and leadership is 'doing the right things.' Nir Bashan has added another crucial element to great leadership: 'having a creator mindset,' which means getting amazing things to happen that would not have happened anyway."

> —Dr. John Scherer, founder of Scherer Leadership
> Center, author of *Facing the Tiger*, and Co-Creator
> of The Adventus Initiative: From Lock-Down to
> Learning and from Re-Set to Renewal

"Reading *The Creator Mindset* was a powerful reminder that fear can either suppress one's ingenuity, or it can fuel it. And that choosing the latter is the key to success. As Nir writes, 'The power of an idea to forever change the outlook of the market you are in is far more powerful than the limitations that you have in front of you.' As both a business owner and a creative director, those words couldn't ring more true. Whether you're just starting out in your career, or you're a veteran in your industry, *The Creator Mindset* will supportively guide you on a journey of introspection that will transform the way you approach problem solving."

> —Mike Wolfsohn, Founder & Chief Creative Officer
> of High, Wide & Handsome

"Fresh insights and tools around innovation are hard to find, but Bashan brings them by the bucketful. Clear and engaging, *The Creator Mindset* shows leaders the importance of embracing change, being open to the 'new,' and making space for bold thinking to happen. Being creative is no longer optional—it's imperative—and this book gets you started."

> —Lisa Bodell, bestselling author of *Why Simple Wins*
> and *Kill the Company*

"Nir's approach to creativity is exactly what the world needs right now. It's the key to innovation, introducing new value to the world beyond building on the iterations of the past. Plus, creativity is literally the fountain of youth!"

—**Brian Solis**, world-renowned digital analyst/
anthropologist and author of *Lifescale*

"Whether you are an entrepreneur or a corporate player, Nir Bashan makes it easy to boost your career, build your brand, and take your product to the next level. Easy and fun to read and impeccably researched, run don't walk, to get this book."

—**Alina Wheeler**, author of *Designing Brand Identity*
and founder of Alina Wheeler Consulting

"While disarming and humorous in style, Bashan demystifies the realm of creative thinking and insists we each harness it as our human birthright. This book goes beyond theory by enlisting readers with provocative exercises and anecdotes so that a creative advantage can be built by anyone interested in improving problem-solving and strategic thinking."

—**Mike Covert**, Co-Founder and CEO of Ignite
Partnership and Co-Founder and Co-CEO of
Capo Commerce

"Nir Bashan's *The Creator Mindset* gives you the tools and inspiration to achieve success through innovation. It's an enjoyable read, packed with engaging stories and practical advice. You'll take away from it a renewed sense of confidence in your own creative potential and ability to flourish in business."

—**Donald Robertson**, author of *How to Think*
Like a Roman Emperor

"Nir Bashan provides an enjoyable and inspirational insight into the power of creative thinking and how we all have the ability to incorporate creativity into our lives and work. Providing an accessible and encouraging approach, this is a must-read for anyone interested in exploring their creative mindset."

—**Chris Griffiths**, bestselling author and
CEO of OpenGenius

"There's only one difference between people who are creative those who are not: mindset. This book will teach you how to become the first type of person."

—**Srinivas Rao**, Chief Creative Instigator and Founder of
Unmistakable Media

"As human beings we are both highly adaptive and driven to explore, create, improvise, and improve the conditions around us. Much of our world today from the paper or tablet upon which you are reading this to, likely, the environment or artifacts around you while you consume this gem are all products of human creativity and imagination. Nir reminds us of that fact and reconnects us with our childhood sense of wonder where nearly anything is possible. *The Creator Mindset* does not only offer why we should all re-engage and develop our innate creativity but, more importantly, simple and approachable means as to how we can unlock our creative potential. In a world of rising technological capabilities with a hyperconnected and interdependent global economy meeting an unprecedented global pandemic, we have never needed human creativity more than we do in this moment to imagine a new and better world for all of us."

—**Heather E. McGowan**, Future of Work strategist and
coauthor of *The Adaptation Advantage*

"Nir's book provides readers with different points of view to unlock their Creator Mindset. It is a valuable piece to help readers relearn how to be creative."

—**David J. Bland**, coauthor of *Testing Business Ideas*

"Creativity is our most valuable asset. I would go so far to say creativity is the currency of our future, especial in unusual and challenging times. Nir Bashan's book and methods will help you to unleash your creative potential in very easy and doable steps. *The Creator Mindset* is especially designed for people who have been out of contact and reach with their inner creative potential. I can highly recommend it."

—**Nicole Srock Stanley**, CEO and Partner at dan pearlman

"*The Creator Mindset* is a practical, wise, and warm approach that blasts away all the mystique and obfuscation that so often surrounds creativity. Filled with engaging practical anecdotes and exercises. I loved the emphasis on positivity and the view that humour is a key element to unlocking creativity. It's something that's not spoken about enough."

—**Fran Luckin**, Chief Creative Officer of Grey, Africa

"In a world of grey, Nir's insight and approach in his book *The Creator Mindset* is a brilliant flash of colour. Thought-provoking and captivating. A true accomplishment."

—**Sean Buckley**, CEO and Founder of Buck Productions

"*The Creator Mindset* is a series of tips and tricks designed to help anyone become more creative. It's friendly and accessible and filled with fodder to help improve creativity no matter the business or career."

—**Jason Sperling**, SVP, Chief of Creative Development, RPA Advertising and author of *Creative Directions*

"Reading *The Creator Mindset* is a journey of self-reflection. The book highlights the fact that better answers exist if you think about things differently. Others will recognize the change in your leadership style when your response to problems is to ask questions and to seek understanding versus providing an answer."

—**Norm Brady**, President & CEO of Associated Builders & Contractors, Inc. Western Michigan Chapter

"What a powerhouse of a book of creative intelligence! Engaging, funny, and perfectly irreverent with plenty of real-world case studies and examples. We are all born creative, and with this book we can capture that long-lost creativity we so deeply desire!"

—**Kimberly Friedmutter**, celebrity hypnotist

"Nir Bashan offers us some powerful and practical tools to bring the force of creativity to what we do. It was wonderful to see how creative he was with a book on creativity. I appreciate his honest disclosure of struggling with most of the tools in his past and the use of excellent stories and examples to bring his tools to life. I encourage you to buy the book to be ready and set with The Creator Mindset."

—**David Zinger**, founder of the Employee Experience & Engagement Network and author of four books on work

"Outstanding, easy, and enjoyable read with invaluable information and strategies to increase your productivity the right way—creatively! Anyone that wants to become more successful and enjoy work more should read this wonderful book. I will be purchasing copies for my staff!"

—**Barry Brockway**, CDR, USN (ret), Innovation Center Director of Operations

"*The Creator Mindset* provides a rich description of creativity and how we all can develop it to create value for us as individuals and businesses. The book provides illustrative stories that underscore the importance of creativity to solving our challenges, taking advantage of opportunities, and staying competitive."

—**Dale Moore,** Founder and President of
The Moore Group LLC and former director of
Naval Air Systems Command (NAVAIR)

"Bashan's book instills a Creator Mindset in anyone who wishes to seek its power. There is no fluff here; just cold, hard accessibility to creativity for all. If you are looking for a no-nonsense guide to improving your creativity for any business or career, this is the book to get."

—**Toby Daniels,** CEO of Crowdcentric

"Bashan's take on creativity and its true power to influence is fantastic. He hits the nail on the head, focusing on the 'how' and 'why' of creativity. It's a fun, factual, and well-researched journey through real-life case studies. It's a great guide to get us back the fundamental value that creativity brings to each of us."

—**Don McNeill,** CEO of DM Inc.

"Bashan is one of those rare thought leaders who offers practical case study advice and does it backed up with loads of careful and meticulous research. I am grateful this book is out there for all to relearn how to be creative."

—**Scott Goodson,** founder and CEO of
StrawberryFrog

"Human beings are designed to create, so businesses that don't welcome creativity lack humanity. *The Creator Mindset* provides an excellent and timely framework to embrace creative thinking and unite the analytical and creative worlds, unlocking human creative potential. We must embrace cognitive diversity across our society and we need not choose between either an analytical or a creative mindset when both are essential to human flourishing."

—**Scott Saunders,** CEO and founder of
HappyMoney Inc.

"Bashan wrote a funny yet poignant book on creativity. And there has never been a better time for this subject. Written in a loving, passionate way, *The Creator Mindset* offers a step-by-step guide on how to improve sales, grow your business, and ultimately become as successful as you wish."

—**Stephen Shapiro,** author of *Invisible Solutions*

"There is a crisis of creativity in business today, but Nir Bashan shows us how to reignite the creator inside all of us."

— **Tim Maleeny,** bestselling author and Chief Strategy
Officer for Havas North America

THE CREATOR MINDSET

MINDSET

92 TOOLS TO UNLOCK THE
SECRETS TO INNOVATION,
GROWTH, AND SUSTAINABILITY

NIR BASHAN

Mc
Graw
Hill

NEW YORK   CHICAGO   SAN FRANCISCO   ATHENS   LONDON   MADRID
MEXICO CITY   MILAN   NEW DELHI   SINGAPORE   SYDNEY   TORONTO

1 2 3 4 5 6 7 8 9   LCR   25 24 23 22 21 20

ISBN 978-1-260-46001-8
MHID   1-260-46001-0

e-ISBN 978-1-260-46002-5
e-MHID   1-260-46002-9

Book Design by Lee Fukui and Mauna Eichner

Library of Congress Cataloging-in-Publication Data

Names: Bashan, Nir, author.
Title: The creator mindset : 92 tools to unlock the secrets to innovation, growth, and sustainability / Nir Bashan.
Description: New York : McGraw Hill, [2020] | Includes bibliographical references and index.
Identifiers: LCCN 2020013677 (print) | LCCN 2020013678 (ebook) | ISBN 9781260460032 (hardback) | ISBN 9781260460025 (ebook)
Subjects: LCSH: Creative ability in business. | Creative thinking. | Problem solving.
Classification: LCC HD53 .B376 2020 (print) | LCC HD53 (ebook) | DDC 658.4/063—dc23
LC record available at https://lccn.loc.gov/2020013677
LC ebook record available at https://lccn.loc.gov/2020013678

The Creator Mindset® is a federally-registered trademark of The Creator Mindset, LLC.

Character illustrations and hand-drawn typeface by Meghan Driscoll and Rebecca Berrington. All art in this book was created for *The Creator Mindset* unless explicitly noted.

McGraw Hill Education books are available at special quantity discounts to use as premiums and sales promotions or for use in corporate training programs. To contact a representative, please visit the Contact Us pages at www.mhprofessional.com.

For Jacob

Contents

Introduction: Logic Alone Is Not Enough   ix

PART I
WHAT IS THE CREATOR MINDSET?

1   Creativity for Noncreative People   3

2   Business Leadership Through an   11
    Unorthodox Channel: Creativity

3   Training Your Mind to Think in a Creative Way   17

4   The Trinity of Creativity   25

PART II
WHY THE CREATOR MINDSET AND WHY NOW?

5   The Brain and Heart on a Collision Course of Prosperity   37

6   When Nothing Else Works, Creativity Will   45

7   A World That Can Be, Not a World That Is   51

PART III
USING THE CREATOR MINDSET

8   Creativity's Unlikely Personality Traits   61

9   On the Virtues of Listening   71

10 The Importance of the Little Victory   77

11 The Value of Making Mistakes   83

12 Art and the Ego   91

13 Character Counts   99

14 The Four Ps You Need for Growth   105

PART IV

SUSTAINING YOUR CREATOR MINDSET

15 The Disease of Self-Doubt   117

16 Comfort, Computers, and the Multitasking Myth 127

17 How to Champion the Good Idea   137

18 The Creator Mindset Guide to Crisis   147

19 The Complacency Conundrum   157

20 Starting Anew   169

    A Closing Note from the Author   179

    Acknowledgments   181

    Notes   187

    Index   195

Logic Alone Is Not Enough

half full

T HERE IS A crisis occurring in most businesses and careers today, and that crisis is a stark lack of creativity. A vast majority of people today have overdeveloped the analytical part of their thinking and underdeveloped the creative part. It doesn't matter what brainpower-enhancing vitamins you're taking or what new healthy diet you're on. It doesn't matter if you have multiple PhDs or shrewd street smarts. The fact remains that the vast majority of people today are operating at half their potential. It's no wonder that sales are lackluster, careers are stalled, and relationships cannot grow.

Unfortunately, it gets worse. A vast majority of companies are operating at half their potential, and most go out of business within the first five years.[1] It's ludicrous. What drives this failure rate? Why are things so bad? Why do most companies fail? The answer is simple, and it's what inspired me to write this book.

The answer is creativity.

The Creator Mindset will teach anyone, including you, how to solve problems through the lens of creativity. It is a method I created to teach anyone how to solve any problem with a blend of both the analytical part and the creative part of the mind, giving you true optimal performance at 100 percent of your potential capacity.

That sounds great, right? But surely someone is teaching this today. Aren't there colleges and courses to teach people how to be creative in business and, by extension, in life?

The answer is, sadly, no, because to be honest, the vast majority of what they teach in business school is analytics. Sure, it's important to have sound analytics and spreadsheet logic, but focusing only on the analytical is a farce. It's simply not good enough. It's like a pilot going to aviation school but learning only how to land or a dentist going to dental school but learning only how to treat bottom teeth. That's what's going on in business schools today. And it's not just schools. This focus on analytics alone affects just about every business today, and it more than likely affects your business too.

The Creator Mindset is the tool you need to embrace creativity *and* utilize analytical thinking in ways that have never been explored.

This shift in thinking is what will make your company and career thrive, and I'll show you how this works in action through case studies of companies that use creativity to thrive. But I have to tell you that there aren't that many. These companies are few and far between. Therefore, it is up to you to go out and forge a new path with The Creator Mindset in your organization or career.

THIS BOOK IS FOR YOU, YES, YOU.

I know you must be thinking, I'm not a creative person, Nir. I don't draw portraits, dance ballet, or play the saxophone. That's just not me. I'm a lawyer or an accountant. I'm an engineer or a nurse. I'm a schoolteacher or a corporate events planner. I'm not a singer or an actor or artist or someone in a creative field. So how will this book help me?

I'll tell you exactly how. *The Creator Mindset* contains insight into the creative mind for those who don't necessarily know they have one. I will teach you how to be creative, but not in the traditional artistic way—in the business way. I find that many people in business don't realize the true power that creativity and creative thought can have in their world. This is what I see with my own eyes over and over while I am out consulting or speaking. People and companies are hungry for a different way, a new way, a creative way.

That is what *The Creator Mindset* is about: bringing out the inner creativity in you to help you solve problems that are unsolvable without a Creator Mindset. Don't worry. I won't teach you how to play an instrument or dance the hula. But I will teach you how to be creative in business because at the end of the day, you have it in you. We all do. It's the spark we are all born with, the spark most of us have extinguished as we've grown older. That spark must be relearned because as adults we are told that creativity is not part and parcel of maturity. It's not serious business acumen. It's frivolous because it cannot be measured and quantified.

But nothing can be further from the truth.

Creativity is in fact essential in *all* you do. This is why we need a fresh perspective. You already have the creative spark in you; you just need to relearn how to use it, and *The Creator Mindset* will show you how.

HOW THIS BOOK WILL HELP YOU

These are the 12 principles we will return to throughout the book:

> *Creativity's Unlikely Personality Traits.* This principle explains how humor, empathy, and courage are the unlikely cornerstones of creativity in business.
>
> *On the Virtues of Listening.* This principle highlights three time-management skills that can be learned only in the context of a creative outlook.
>
> *The Importance of the Little Victory.* Often, we are led to believe that big victories are the only ones that matter. But our attention should be focused instead on how to envision our goals creatively in small chunks.
>
> *The Value of Making Mistakes.* Mistake utility is a view found only in creativity in which a mistake becomes lucrative. Here we look at how mistakes can benefit your company and career.
>
> *Art and the Ego.* The gap between creativity and art is huge, and so are our egos from time to time. We must learn the difference to keep ego from taking over.
>
> *Character Counts.* Three creative tools will help your career or business when times get tough, which they always do.

The Four Ps You Need for Growth. My four Ps of business will help anyone embrace creativity collectively at every step of my program.

The Disease of Self-Doubt. This principle shows us how to use creativity to fight one of humanity's most destructive behaviors.

Comfort, Computers, and the Multitasking Myth. Technology and comfort work in concert to decrease creativity. This principle helps you understand how to resist comfort and limit technology so that creativity can bloom.

How to Champion the Good Idea. This principle highlights five ways to find what is trapping and limiting creativity in your career or organization and then how to free it.

The Creator Mindset Guide to Crisis. In the face of a terrible tragedy in 1982 came an accidental road map to creativity that we can use today.

The Complacency Conundrum. This principle is illustrated by case studies about companies that were creative but then got complacent. It shows what we can learn from their mistakes about how to keep from getting complacent in our careers or businesses.

Through these simple principles you will learn to reference each day, you will begin to awaken your own Creator Mindset. And as you gain comfort with thinking creatively, you will see a new approach to a genuine authenticity that most professionals and businesses want but few know how to achieve. This authenticity is revealed through the lens of creativity.

You will learn in these pages how to achieve the holy grail of innovation. It's not those lightbulb moments of inspiration or secret sorcery that create innovation. Instead, innovation is something you can learn to create. It's something that can be taught. I will show you how.

THE COST OF CREATIVITY

I know what else you might be thinking: Ah! But this is going to be expensive. I bet most of The Creator Mindset tools aren't cheap.

But the truth is that every tool in this book—every single one—costs you nothing. Absolutely nothing. They are all free to use: no licensing, no royalties, nothing. Just free. Other than the cost of the book (and maybe a workshop or keynote that I give at your company or convention), implementing these creative principles will cost you nothing. How cool is that? But like anything in life, there is a catch. Here's the thing: not using these tools and techniques can cost you everything.

You see, the stakes are high today. In an ultracompetitive global economy, there is only one chance to get it right. And as the economy shifts from the industrial economy of yesteryear to the new idea economy of tomorrow, it is imperative that we be armed with the ability to create ideas readily and frequently. The future of your brand, whether it's your personal brand, a start-up, a restaurant, or a Fortune 500 firm, depends on your ability to connect with your audience emotionally and convincingly. No matter what it is that you do, from doctor to banker, from regulator to electrician, from veterinarian to controller, *The Creator Mindset* is a must-read. You will learn to connect emotionally and convincingly with your chosen audience.

I'm going to predict your thinking again. It is something along the lines of this: Come on, Nir. Really? I run a roofing business. Why do I need any of this creative stuff? Am I right? If you are thinking like this, the truth of the matter is that through the lens of creativity you will find your audience. And if you can connect with your audience, you will create business opportunities. And if you create business opportunities, you will increase your bottom line. It really is that simple when you're armed with The Creator Mindset.

Perhaps you are an employee who is trying to get ahead. You're working hard day after day, putting in more hours than the rest, consistently hitting the mark. Yet time and time again you hit a ceiling, unable to climb any higher, unable to achieve your goals, wondering why you can't get ahead. The bottom line is that without creativity you cannot scale new heights and reach your chosen destiny.

You might be tempted to think that creativity is all about an advertisement or your business card or website design. Although that certainly is important, it's necessary to dive much deeper into unfamiliar ways to harness creativity in all you do. I know this different way of looking at things may be scary at first, but it ultimately will open you up to new and exciting opportunities never before seen.

Your life will change forever because you will understand how to use creative principles to solve everyday problems, and not just at work. You literally will learn to change the function of your brain to incorporate creativity, and in doing so you will see the world as you've never seen it before.

We tend to devalue creative solutions in modern life. It's too flimsy. It's something that's too out there. It's artsy-fartsy. We roll our eyes. It's probably for someone else because I'm not that smart or funny or artistic. But the truth is that it's not for someone else. *It's for you.* This way of thinking will help you and be of service to you and your goals. The brain is divided into two hemispheres—logical and creative—and this book will help you bridge the gap between them so that you can achieve magnificent harmonious success.

The creative mind is one that is not subject to limitations. The creative mind sees what can be rather than what is. How incredibly powerful is that? Just think about it for a second. Take a moment and look at this book closely. I mean it. Stick your finger on this page to hold your place and then look at the front and back covers. Admire them from different angles. Did we do a good job on the cover? Do you like it? Perhaps you can think of another way to lay out the print. Does this typeface look good? Is it hard to read? Simply looking at something as it *can be* rather than *as it is* can change the very nature of the problem you are thinking about right now as you read these words on the page.

Creativity will teach you to see things as they should be, not as they are. A plumber goes to a house and encounters a clogged sink. You see putrid water and a horrible situation, but the plumber sees opportunity and a chance to be of service. On these pages you will learn to see the world as you think it should be, not as it is.

One of the great things about thinking creatively is that it gives you the opportunity to see things in different ways. This is evident because the creative mind cannot see any boundaries to its thinking. It behaves and adapts in such a way that nothing can stop it. Not even reality. Not even a lack of resources. Not even your current crappy cash flow situation or low salary. That is why the creative mind is so important. Imagine a tool in the business world that can uplift you in even the most desolate circumstances by making you believe that there is opportunity in each obstacle.

Forever the optimist, The Creator Mindset will enable you to dream, to fly, to conquer, to solve, to live. Often a third-class citizen compared with other pressing business needs or ignored altogether, The Creator Mindset can supersede all limitations and be more useful than almost anything else.

When your thinking has no barriers, your potential has no barriers.

I wrote this book for you because I'm tired of all these business leaders who are keeping that creativity to themselves. They pretend that it cannot be learned. They say things like "I've got it and you don't." Whatever "it" is. They keep creativity under lock and key away from the general public for fear of revealing their intellectual property. But creativity is far too valuable to humanity to be controlled by just a few people. It is possible to learn it. The pages of this book will show you how. This is a deeply personal undertaking years in the making because the time has come for creativity to be used by anyone who seeks its power.

PART 1

WHAT IS THE CREATOR MINDSET?

An Overview of the
Creative Revolution About
to Take Place in Business

Creativity for
Noncreative People

kid nir

STARTED MY FIRST company when I was nine years old. I mean calling it a company is probably a very generous description. My friend Richard and I needed money to fund a very serious pursuit: we needed to buy baseball cards and fast food, which when you're nine years old is a big deal. Our families were living paycheck to paycheck and could not afford to hand out any extra money, and so we knew that we had to take action ourselves.

Richard and I started a company with the operating agreement of a handshake. We had stumbled on what we thought was the best idea in the world, something that would bring in limitless amounts of money and make us rich beyond our wildest dreams: we were going to go door-to-door washing cars.

We quickly raided the garage and kitchen for supplies. We used hand soap as car-washing soap. He found a bucket. I had a ratty old hose that leaked. His mom had thrown out a vacuum cleaner that was putting out more smoke than anything else and barely sucked anything in. But none of that mattered because our plan was perfect. We put our inventory together and found that we had just enough supplies for our first wash. All we needed was that first client.

It wasn't easy because we had no idea what we were doing. How could we get someone to let us wash a car for money? It was a high mountain to climb. Our second hurdle? How much to charge clients. We had no idea what we could get for a car wash. Twenty dollars? Two dollars? What would people pay for this service? We were clueless. Our third hurdle? If they opened the door, what would we say? How would that work? Who would talk first, me or Richard? It was far too much to figure out in advance, and so we did what any kid would have done in our case: we jumped in blind. We would figure it out along the way. We thought, Hey, what can possibly go wrong?

Off we went door-to-door to face countless rejections. Doors slammed. People thought we were nuts. Two kids knocking on a door with a hodgepodge of cleaning supplies saying that they wanted to wash your car? Who could blame people for slamming the door? And we were asking people to hand over their car keys!

Richard and I sat on the sidewalk after an entire day of hearing "no, no, no." It was a dark moment. All seemed lost. But soon all our thoughts turned to figuring out how we needed *just* one person to say yes, and after that the floodgates to wealth would open. I will never forget it as long as I live. It was a late Saturday afternoon, and my best friend looked at me and asked, "What now?"

It was a defining moment of my youth that set me up to be the man I am today. Life is full of critical "what now" moments, and the way you *react* means far more than what has *happened*.

This was a critical juncture in which a choice had to be made— a creative choice.

It was then and there that I was forced to decide what to do. And those decisions bred the first seeds of a lifetime of developing, tweaking, and tinkering with a formula that today I call The Creator Mindset. It's a way of thinking that I am certain will change your life forever. I know because it has certainly changed mine and those of my clients all over the world: JetBlue, Microsoft, the NFL, EA Sports, American Airlines, AT&T, and many, many others.

The Creator Mindset introduces a new way of thinking that is not taught anywhere else. Some folks already "have it," and you probably know a few of them. It's that business owner who put out a coupon and got a host of new clients. It's that engineering firm that did a big pro bono job and then secured a host of new accounts. It's the company that gives you points for every dollar you spend and then gives away its product or service for free. All these examples make you think, How did he or she or they think of that? I wish I could do that. Well, the time for wishing and wanting is over. It's time to get serious about training your mind to think creatively, and that's exactly what this book and program will teach you.

The first and most important step in this process is believing one thing: *everything about creativity can be learned.*

Far too many people believe deep down that they're not creative. I see it often when giving keynotes or consulting with clients. It depresses me because folks always think that it is someone else who's creative—never them. Perhaps you are one of those people who believe that they are not creative. But understanding the concept that creativity is a *tool*—a tool like any other—will go a long way. And understanding that creativity can be learned just like anything else will put your mind at ease.

You can learn how to think creatively. It's just that so little time and energy is spent on developing a road map to teach creativity as a tool. We are programmed to develop the analytical mind through the many institutions that exist today to propel analytical agendas. We as a society have shifted away from the creative mind—and at shocking peril.

For instance, we see this as clear as day when it comes to medicine. Modern medicine is so concerned with the physical instead of the mental because it's much easier to mend a broken bone than it is to mend a broken mind.[1] Broken bones and physical injuries are tangible; we can see, feel, and touch them, and that is comfortable, familiar, and apparent. It's simple to prove this and say to others: Look, I fixed the broken arm. But you cannot show someone that you've improved a person's way of thinking. Creativity is the same. It's marginalized simply because quantification of creativity isn't possible.[2]

I'm here to show you that you *can* see creativity just as clearly as you see sales at the end of the quarter. You just need to train your mind to be able to see in a different way. I know that this is a revolution in thinking, and I think it's fair to say that you're probably starting to doubt this, but I need you to stick with me. Sure, this might represent a departure from where you feel comfortable and from what is familiar, but that's okay. Why? Because as you will learn later in this book, comfort isn't all it's cracked up to be.

■   ■   ■

OUT OF ALL ANIMALS on earth, we have been bestowed with the most amazing device that has ever been created. Not our sense of sight. Not our sense of smell. Not even our opposable thumbs (although having an opposable thumb is pretty awesome). Instead, the most impressive device that we have as humans is the brain. And what makes the human brain unique is its ability to be both logical and creative, which really are two ways of thinking that are as different as anything can be. Yet amazingly they live together within our brains! In one place. How incredible.

This power to alternate our thinking between the analytical and the creative[3] at will may seem unimpressive at first, but it makes us unique because we are the only animals on earth that can do it. It gives us the ability to move creativity forward[4] in our thoughts, and this is important to realize because The Creator Mindset really does introduce a revolutionary biological shift in the brain.

In recent decades, scientists have uncovered a phenomenon in the human brain known as neuroplasticity.[5,6] This amazing discovery has taught us that our brains literally can change. New synapses can connect as we take on new knowledge, neurons throughout the brain can break old connections and make new ones, and brand-new cells are always being created.[7] This shift to thinking about the brain as a changing organism is revolutionary because until these discoveries were made, most scientists thought that the brain was fixed, meaning that after childhood the brain remained unchanged and was unable to learn something new. But we now know that this is not the case. It turns out that the brain has the ability to change throughout our lives almost on the fly as it learns and interprets new information. Think about that for a moment. How incredibly powerful is that? All it takes to activate this change is the will to learn something new. The declaration that you make today while reading these words on this printed page (or tablet or while listening to audio) can change your life profoundly.

Theodor Herzl said, "If you will it, it is no dream."[8] Turns out he was right. You just have to will it. This knowledge you accept can exercise your brain into new and different levels of fitness. The structure of the brain will change as it ingests new and different ways to learn, to solve problems, and to grow. It turns out that indeed you can teach an old dog new tricks.[9] And not only that: our brains can physically rearrange themselves according to the input to which we are exposed.

Knowledge that we ingest physically changes the way our brains function. In describing the history of our understanding of neuroplasticity, Nicholas Carr writes, "The brain's plasticity is not limited to the somatosensory cortex, the area that governs our sense of touch. It's universal. Virtually all of our neural circuits— whether they're involved in feeling, seeing, hearing, moving, thinking, learning, perceiving, or remembering—are subject to change."[10]

This is good news on several fronts. It means that we can literally hardwire our brains to accept other ways of thinking,[11] including a way of thinking creatively.[12] There is nothing that cannot be learned.

This discovery came at the perfect time in our history. Today, it's more important than ever because the analytical side of our brains has been on overload for far too long. It has been besotted with the love of quantification, multitasking, technology, data, and more. We are so heavily skewed toward the analytical that the creative part of the brain has been left to wither away like a plant that is not watered. We are not operating in the most optimal way possible. But with this new science, there is hope.

■ ■ ■

THE CREATOR MINDSET REPRESENTS a correction in the way the brain has been functioning. Like a real estate market that is out of whack and must recalibrate to current trends, our heavily skewed way of thinking is in dire need of correcting to be able to deal with our realities in the twenty-first century. But to be clear, I am not suggesting that you throw away all that has worked for you thus far and gotten you to where you are today. Analytical skills are important. However, in isolation they are damaging. Without uniting the analytical and the creative, we are operating on a half tank of gas. We're never really using our full potential, always wondering why we are not happy, wondering why we aren't there yet.

But as we begin to unite the analytical and the creative, we learn how to be a more effective leader, how to improve our bottom line, how to get ahead to that next promotion. We begin to create an environment that is ripe for opportunity, growth, and expansion in our market.[13] On top of all of that, it just might make you a better person.

■ ■ ■

AS WE WRAP UP this chapter, let's return to where Richard and I left off. We had no customers, but we had determination as we sat on that curb figuring out our next step. We were in search of something—anything—to save our business. In that moment, it occurred to me that we had to get creative in order to survive.

Ultimately, I decided to package our fledgling business as a customer service operation. Sure, we would wash your car, but we also would throw away all the junk on your lawn or porch. We would empty out the trash from your house and put out the cans on the curb. We would clean out and organize your car's trunk. We would top off your windshield wiper fluid with soapy water. We would do extra things that are not necessarily related to car washing. And with that, we found a sales pitch rhythm when going door-to-door. We would sing little rhymes like "Junk in your trunk, not any more. Nir and Richard will wash your car for sure!" when folks opened the door. Sure, now it's embarrassing, but at the time it worked.

We discovered that neighbors would purchase a car wash from us for different reasons. Some wanted to help out two kids. Some had a dirty car. Some hated hauling out the trash bins or cleaning off the porch. But ultimately folks were willing to pay a fair price of $5 a pop for services, some of which included washing a car. Sure, we got stiffed a few times, which was terrible and stung, but our customers and their concerns set up a lifetime of learning how to address problems from a creative perspective for me.

I know what you're thinking: This creative stuff is neat, but how can it help me in my business? I have real deadlines, real inventory, real customers. And I need a plan for how to grow and improve my business to achieve very specific goals. And none of those goals are "creative." They are real fiscal objectives and thus need to be treated with gravity.

But I am here to argue that no matter what your goals are, without creativity you are merely operating your business like everyone else: set in the analytical without the benefit of the creative. No matter how optimal your thinking is, you are running the business at 50 percent of your available brainpower. Think about that for a minute. You are running your business at best on *only half* of your potential. Would you accept an invoice paid for 50 percent of the full amount? Or a vendor delivering 50 percent of the job? Or half your paycheck? Of course not. I know you wouldn't, and neither would I. But that's exactly what you are doing today and every day as you neglect 50 percent of your brain. Now is the time to activate it, so let's get moving.

2

Business Leadership Through an Unorthodox Channel: Creativity

steve + bill

DID YOU KNOW that Steve Jobs once was ousted from Apple by a board whose members thought that they could run the company better than he could?[1] It's true, and as a result, there was a time when the company was failing miserably. Steve kept trying to get back in, but he had little luck. The new leadership at Apple led with an analytical mindset. The quest for innovation had dried up, and the search turned to maximizing margins and other analytical goals. Their products that had potential were left alone to founder.[2] Without any product updates, attention, or changes, the new leadership was stuck in "If it ain't broke, why fix it?" mode. They were ignoring one of the most fundamental tenets of The Creator Mindset: *change is one of the only things you can count on.*

Competitors started to make better products. People looked to Apple to change and grow, to innovate and create, but instead they released same old model after same old model. This was very similar to what Detroit's Big Three were doing in the early and middle 1980s while the Japanese were in better touch with what the automotive consumer was looking to buy.[3] Apple wasn't adopting The Creator Mindset, which looks at stagnation the same way it views death. If you're not continuously looking to foster an environment that breeds creativity, you will be relegated to the pages of history.

Board meeting after board meeting at Apple yielded no results, and soon enough bankruptcy was nearing and a decision had been made: Apple was going to do a massive layoff.[4]

This shouldn't be surprising because the analytical mindset always looks to numbers for answers. And what better number to look at than payroll? We need to cut staff to stay profitable, right? It's an analytical strategy as old as time. It was imperative in yesterday's economy, which operated strictly on quantification.

In the end, cutting payroll failed, so they needed the next big things: "cost cutting" and "restructuring" were the new way to save the company. Spoiler alert: These options are hardly innovative management techniques. In fact, they're tools that you're probably already familiar with. Sure, there may be parts of these techniques that help (temporarily), but *any gain without creativity is short-lived*. That is why massive layoffs almost never work. That is why restructuring has never really kept up with change. I'm sure you can come up with some of your own analytical tools that appear to work briefly but stop working at some point. That is the case because thinking with only analytics and ignoring the creative most often leads to failure. What you're really doing is treating the symptoms instead of looking for a cure.

After those attempts failed, the board at Apple decided on the last of the analytical trump cards: suing someone. In this case, that was Microsoft. This was the big move, the big shake-up. They thought, This is sure to work! You see, at that time Microsoft was employing a user interface in Windows that looked a lot like the user interface in Apple's system. It had similar icons, a similar look and feel, and a similar user experience with a mouse and a keyboard to control things that were happening on the screen. Because we are all so computer-literate these days, those things seem commonplace, but at that time they were not.

Finally, as a last resort, Steve Jobs was allowed to rejoin the company he had started. With Apple facing bankruptcy by the end of the year, most thought that there was nothing that could be done. But that was because the mindset at Apple was stuck in the analytical. And just as you need more than one tool to build a house, you need more than one tool to solve problems in your business. Steve Jobs knew this intuitively. He knew that the analytical was nothing without the creative, and so he had a revolutionary creative idea: he was going to go to Bill Gates at Microsoft and ask him to bail out Apple.[5]

In case you don't know the backstory, Apple and Microsoft were enemies at that time, and the relationship between Bill Gates and Steve Jobs was complicated at best. Sure, they had been friends briefly in the 1970s, but their friendship had been strained by their competition. They both created very similar products under very different brands.

You can only imagine the jeers, sarcasm, and anger this idea generated at Apple. The lawyers were outraged. The board was aghast. Most people at Apple thought that Steve Jobs had lost his mind. But what Jobs did was combine the analytical and the creative to come up with an idea. The analytical side showed him that his company was about to go bankrupt, and the creative side showed him that the solution just might come from the most unlikely of sources.

He met with Bill Gates, but the details of the meeting are not well recorded. It was a conversation between two bitter rivals, two former friends. Yet the result of the meeting changed the history of the technology sector forever. Bill Gates did indeed make a $150 million investment in Apple at a time when it was needed most, with the one condition being that Apple drop the lawsuit. Steve Jobs agreed.[6]

The reverberations of this bailout have been felt ever since. Steve Jobs didn't just win here; Bill Gates did too. He *also* made a creative decision by believing that having major competition—a fierce rival—was actually good for business.

I remember early in my career battling competition and trying to stay in business. And a mentor of mine told me that he loved competition and that I should learn to love it too. I thought this was silly because I wanted to crush my competition and be on top, but I eventually learned that he was right. Competition makes your offerings better. It forces you to stay adept and in touch with your consumers. Plus, it's good for consumers to have a choice.

It turned out that both Apple and Microsoft did very well after a leap of faith taken on creativity. This is not an idea that any analytical mindset would have produced. Too often the credit goes only to Steve Jobs in this story, but Bill Gates also took on a Creator Mindset in that he recognized that the thinking of yesterday will not be the same as the thinking of tomorrow.

■   ■   ■

THE REASON I TELL this story is simple. It's my hope that if we are armed with The Creator Mindset, these stories of creative triumphs in business will become more and more commonplace. We need these stories because they appeal to us on a human level. They are full of compassion, empathy, connectivity, and drive, and they are just plain awesome. They make us feel warm and fuzzy because they tap into a human element that is central to the DNA of who we are: the creative. No one gets warm and fuzzy over the analytical, the spreadsheet logic, the rigidity of reason. But when you tap into an emotional nerve, that gets us going. It moves us in a way that only creativity can. It turns out that this DNA actually kept us from being eaten by creatures far more analytically complex than us in our prehistoric past, but that's a story for later in the book.

Looking at the case study of Apple, we see that there was a lot of risk taken on thinking creatively that's uncomfortable for most people to engage in. But this is not wanton risk taking or reckless abandon; this is the calculated risk that creativity can bring. It is a welcome departure from the tried-and-true responses to crisis that have been executed in business forever with dubious results: responses such as downsizing and restructuring. All of that was tried in this story, but none of it worked.

I wish that stories like this one were commonplace, but in fact they're not. That's one of the reasons I wrote this book. Most people are in awe of Steve Jobs and what he was able to do at Apple, and they called him creative. It is a rightful honor, but imagine unlocking the secrets that Steve Jobs used at Apple so that they are readily available for you to use as well. It can be done through the lens of creativity no matter what it is that you do. In your business, in your industry, and in your life, The Creator Mindset codifies what has been unable or unwilling to be codified until now. It's the creativity option in your business that you are now learning how to activate.

■   ■   ■

GOOD LEADERSHIP RELIES ON sound business acumen. But what if that acumen has forever been changed? What if the practices of yesterday are not relevant to the practices of tomorrow? The Creator Mindset is forcing old theories of economics, management, and "best practices" to be rapidly replaced with a new way of thinking. This way of thinking introduces possibilities that were never there before. They introduce a new creative idea economy that relies on the activation of a long-ignored part of the mind that you are learning to activate now.

Training Your Mind to Think in a Creative Way

painting

O NE OF MY earliest memories is from kindergarten. It's fairly normal and might be seen as routine, but to me it was a defining moment of my young childhood education that I still remember vividly.

I was given a *huge* piece of butcher paper. I still remember the smell, the brown color, the texture, the feel, and the fact that it was bigger than my entire desk. Up to that point, I had never seen a piece of paper that big.

Soon the teacher gave every student in the class a paintbrush and a few different colors. She told us to fill the paper with a drawing of anything we wanted. It was my introduction to art, which is where most people are introduced to creativity. I remember a distinct feeling washing over me. It was a feeling of possibility, a feeling of freedom, and a feeling that nothing else mattered except the huge canvas in front of me, along with the excitement of all the possibilities I could come up with to fill it. That piece of paper was almost like a window into the imagination. I remember instantly thinking that anything could happen.

I viewed that piece of paper as a child, and I saw what *could be*, not what *was*. This moment had nothing to do with art per se. It had nothing to do with painting. It had to do with the fact that I was faced with a world of possibility.

I was not stuck on things that I now might see as an adult with an analytical mindset, such as obstacles, excuses, or lack of resources. I was not thinking about how I didn't have the fanciest paintbrush or years of training or enough time or money. None of that mattered. I wasn't thinking the way adults do. I was thinking like a child, and all that mattered to me were the endless possibilities of what I could do.

As children, we are encouraged to explore our creativity. Sometimes this happens in a traditional art sense of drawing or painting or whatever. But not always. Even more important than in traditional art, creativity is seen in just about everything a child does to solve problems. Whether it's though toys or play or just imagination, children are more inclined to creativity and attempting to use creativity as a solution to problems in all that they do.[1] As children we were given blocks to play with, and we built up those blocks to be a fortresses or castles that lived in our imagination. We then took them apart and built bridges from one toy to another. We took anything we could find—kitchen utensils, pots, and pans—and made the most fantastic worlds possible. We took couch cushions and built secret passageways around the living room—a passageway though the universe. Our imagination was not restrained; instead, it flourished.

But as adults we find ourselves relying on the practical and analytical. What in hell happened to get us here? I bet that if I gave you a piece of butcher paper or some blocks, you wouldn't know what to do with them. The thought of seeing a couch cushion as anything other than a couch cushion seems to us to be preposterous. Why would we do that? It's just something to sit on. Yet when we were children, these things and others were opportunities to create—to see things as they can be, not as they are. We have forgotten what it is like to taste the freedom that comes with creative thought and take the weight of unrelenting reason off our backs. Again, this is not about drawing or painting or art. It's about creativity and giving yourself the freedom to look at the world as it could be, not what your skeptical adult mind tells you it is.

I'd like for you to grab a piece of paper, any piece of paper around you. If you don't have one available, you can use this book as your paper. Next, grab a pen. Go on; I will wait. Got it? Great.

Now I want you to draw a picture of a flower in the margin of this book or on your piece of paper. I mean it: go ahead and draw something. I know that you might not be an artist. I am no artist myself. But that doesn't matter. I've done this exercise in workshops all over the world. Believe me: your artistic ability matters none. No matter how big or small you draw your flower, I just want you to draw. Feel your hand moving over the paper. Feel the funny tickling as you draw lines instead of the shapes of letters. Feels kind of good, doesn't it? Feels relaxing. Or at least different. Now I want you to take a picture of the flower and post it to our Instagram page, using the hashtag #thecreatormindset.

I want this to be your first commitment to living The Creator Mindset. No matter how bad your flower might look. Because at the end of the day, it really doesn't matter how it looks. It just matters that you try. And really, trying is just practice. It is a practice that builds muscle memory just like working out or learning a new language.

The Creator Mindset is a training regimen that relies on you exercising the connections in your brain to see a different way forward, a creative way forward. It's not about the flower. It's not about the art. It's about the commitment and the will to begin to see the world creatively.

■   ■   ■

WE DON'T NEED TO learn how to be creative. We need to *relearn* how to be creative. One thing you can try right this minute is think about a persistent problem that's eating away at you. It can be that your business is failing or struggling in one particular area. It could be the promotion you are after and are not getting. Think about that problem and make sure it's clear in your mind.

Now we will work together to rewire the structure of your brain to think creatively, and I will help you awaken your long-lost creativity.

Go ahead and pick up the same pen, but this time write down the issue you're thinking about in the margin of the book. I really need you to write it down because thinking about it is not enough. Now I want you to look at the problem you wrote down. Look at the words you have written. Look at the shape of the letters. What do the letters look like? Block letters? Cursive? Uppercase? Lowercase? Now study the look of the letters as you've never done before. See how each line connects. See how big or small the letters are of the problem or issue you have written down.

Remember, you are now relearning how to think creatively, so take your time. I am sure that no matter who you are or how far away from a Creator Mindset you are, you will begin to see associations with the word you wrote down that spark some type of thought. Don't bury it the way you normally do! Think about what is popping into your mind right now as you read these words. Are you thinking of something unrelated? Something that has nothing to do with the problem? Great! You are starting to look at the issue creatively. Are you thinking of what you wrote down? Great! You are starting to look at things creatively. Let any and all thoughts wander into your brain and do not edit them because that is your childhood creativity trying to come back out. There is a creative solution for any issue, no matter what it is. You just have to listen.

Now I want you to try listening to the voice in your head that occasionally pops up with something new—something fresh. Listen to the voice that you have shut down for some reason or another. It's the creative side of the brain that you have shut down for so long trying to help you solve problems creatively just as it did when you were a child. And as with children, it turns out that before any analytical skills are developed, the first skills are creative problem-solving skills.[2] These are the skills that develop before language, before fine motor skills. They develop earlier than anything else because they are a key facet of why humans

survived while other animals perished. We will get into more details on human survival later, but for now know that we are all
born with a creative voice, and listening to what that voice is telling you is priceless. This usually comes across as a crazy idea
that you don't share or execute because you worry about what
might happen. Or it could be an idea that strikes you in bed at
night just before you fall asleep and you see it as totally radical.
It could be something you encounter while doing creativity exercises that strikes you as too crazy. You shove it down because it's
too wild. It's not comfortable. Or worst of all, you worry about
what people might think.

What is happening here is that the creativity we are all born
with is trying to get through the thick concrete barrier of the
analytical you have worked so hard all your life to build. Often, sadly, it cannot get through. You kill the idea before it has a
chance to fly. You deem it too "out there," too crazy. But just like
Steve Jobs's idea of going to his archrival to ask for a bailout, it
just might work.

But this involves change, and I realize as I give talks all over
the world that change is one of the most difficult constructs of
the human condition to deal with. Everyone hates change. No
matter where in the world I visit, it's the same. We are built to accept patterns in our day, our lives, our work, and our relationships. Even biologically we are prone to patterns in all that we
do. Anything that threatens the status quo is seen as a threat to
our well-being.[3]

That is why my technique is so easy. It is not about memori-
zation or some 13-step protocol that costs a lot of money or requires new equipment. The Creator Mindset method is focused
on awakening your long-lost ability to think creatively to solve
any problem. Because you already have it in you, you just need to
relearn how to listen to it. Most of us have shut off that voice or

ignored it by not listening to it. We need to listen to it. Just being conscious of that fact will enable us to listen to the creative part of the mind when it pops up. And it will pop up. It might be in five seconds or five weeks from now (heaven forbid), but it will pop up. Now is the time to make the choice to listen.

It all comes down to a choice between continuing with the same old results that limit us or embracing change and finally arriving at the optimal blend of human performance: the uniting of the creative and the analytical.

The Creator Mindset wills a world where everything is possible and nothing is impossible. It's a world where possibility exists instead of limitations. Imagine putting that power to work on your business or career. The Creator Mindset unleashes potential, not limitations. We all have it deep within us. It's a matter of learning how to reawaken it. One of the guideposts of living the life of The Creator Mindset is learning how to retrain our minds to think like a child again. You are doing that right now, just as we did in the flower-drawing exercise and the study of your handwriting. It turns out that even innovation itself can be learned because it is a subset of creativity with three simple steps: what I call the Trinity of Creativity.

CHAPTER

4

The Trinity of Creativity

pizza guy

THROUGHOUT HISTORY, CREATIVITY has been shrouded in mystery. It is a realm only a few can access that forever shuts the rest of us out, a calling so high and noble that it is unobtainable by mere mortals. We are taught over and over that creativity is something you cannot learn. It is something you either have or don't have. Those who have it possess some kind of otherworldly wisdom and grace that we can only wish we had.

The worst myth is that creativity relies on "inspiration." In this view, the stars must align, and only then will inspiration strike in that special way; it's something fleeting that happens only so often. We are told that inspiration is a limited resource that you will run out of one day. You will be forever bereft of a creative way to think as your finite supply of inspiration shrivels up and dies.

The truth is that all of those things are complete and utter baloney. Creativity is something that *can* be taught and moreover can be relearned, just as you are doing today. As you begin to

25

awaken your long-lost inner creativity, you will need a formula to enable repeatable success no matter what business you are in or what you do. My Trinity of Creativity will guide you and your company to creative success. It will deliver the "how" that I believe is critical for all to see. The three points are what I call the *Concept*, the *Idea*, and the *Execution*. Let's look a bit closer at each one individually and then see how they combine to create a powerful tool.

Take a look at Figure 4.1. At the top, you have the Concept, which is the widest view. Then, as we move toward the middle of the chart, we have the Idea. Notice how things get more and more focused and more and more defined as we go lower in the chart. Finally, as we get to the bottom, we have the Execution, the distilled essence of the process.

FIGURE 4.1

The Creative Process

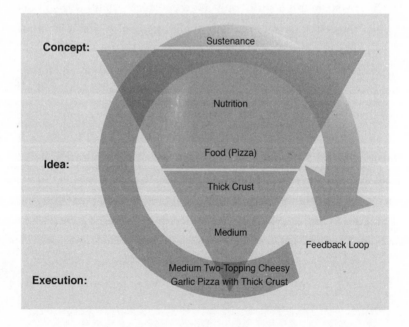

THE CONCEPT

To get started, I want you to imagine the perspective of a satellite up in space looking at the Earth. What can you see from up that high? You probably see clouds, weather, the shapes of the continents, water, and more. This is the widest view of the Earth possible, but you can't zoom in to see details. This view is what I call the Concept.

In applying the Concept to business, you take on the highest-level view of your career or business possible. Here you can see trends come and go. You can see where the company or your career should be headed several years into the future. You can see big-picture items but are not so good at seeing medium-level things, much less any details. This is the widest and highest perspective possible in which to frame your career or company.

For example, if you are a company that manufactures cars, the Concept could be *mobility* or *transportation*. There really is no "right" answer; it is whatever makes the most sense to you.

If you are looking at your career in, say, nursing, you might say that the Concept of your career is *communication* because keeping patients informed throughout their journey is the highest-level view of your job possible. Or you might say that *care* is the Concept of your career because what you do is care for people in different ways.

There is no right or wrong answer for the Concept of your career or business. The Concept needs to be what feels the best for you in your particular situation, and it needs to stay pretty broad but also important enough that you will stand behind it. Therefore, the Concept is the most significant category that your career or company encompasses. In a rush to identify your particular Concept, you may be tempted to take a shortcut and get too specific, but in identifying your Concept, you give your career or company the broadest meaning possible. What part of your career or company gives you the most meaning? That is your Concept.

> I'd like you to do a brief exercise by writing down what the Concept of your business or career is. I'd like you to write it in the margins of this page or somewhere close by. Write down the Concept of your business or career in a word or a few words that encompass the highest level of meaning for you on what it is that you do. Write it down and circle it.

THE IDEA

Now that we have identified the Concept of your career or business, it is time to look at the next building block in my formula for making creativity happen. The Idea is a medium-level view that makes the Concept a bit more specific. Think of this as a street view that reveals far more details, almost like holding a camera and looking through it onto the street. With this view, details come into focus. We can see plants, animals, and people, all of which were impossible to see in the Concept satellite view.

When you apply the Idea view in your career or business, you can see more of the day-to-day details of what is going on. Think about hour-to-hour, week-to-week, and month-to-month interactions. You cannot see trends or patterns or the far outlook, but you sure can see what is going on in front of you!

The Idea will always follow the Concept as a more refined derivative of the Concept. Just as the Concept carries the most meaning to you, the Idea will carry the most practical view of your career or business. In the case of the nurse, your Idea is most likely a *head nurse* or a *pediatric nurse*. It further narrows your role down into the Idea but does not fully narrow it down into a lot of detail.

> Below where you have written your Concept and cir-cled it, I'd like you to write your Idea. There is no right or wrong Idea for your career or business; there is only what feels right to you. Write it down in the mar-gin and circle it.
>
> You may be tempted to get superspecific, but please resist that urge for now. The Idea should be a midlevel perspective of your company or career. It's more or less what you tell someone who asks you what you do at a party.

THE EXECUTION

Finally, we have the Execution, which consists of the nitty-gritty details of the business. This is the electron-microscopic view. Here you can see nothing but the details and the minute-to-minute actions of your business or career. Here you can see, as the seconds of the clock go ticking by, the action, the drama, and the deep details of your everyday work.

If the Concept is the high-level view and the Idea is the mid-level view, the Execution is the view from deep within the trench. This consists of the constant fires that need to be put out and the everyday grievances of the staff. As is true when you look into a microscope, here we can see only the exact atoms, not the whole object the atoms make up.

For our nursing example, the Execution might be a *neonatal intensive care unit nurse*. It is the very specific Execution of your career as a derivative of the Idea and the Concept.

> Below where you have written and circled your Concept and have written and circled your Idea, I'd like for you to write and circle your Execution. There is no right or wrong Execution to your career or business; there is only what feels right to you. It's a very specific item, a laser-focused definition of what it is that your company offers or what you do in your career. Write it down in the margin.
>
> Be as detailed as possible. It is something you tell people after meeting them at a party and they show interest in what you do.

PUTTING THEM TOGETHER

All three views are critical for a business to function successfully with The Creator Mindset. It may be tempting to stay in the view you are most comfortable in, but to master the task of infusing creativity into your business, you must have visibility into all three.

Most of us are comfortable in only one of the views, and usually that view is the Execution: the electron-microscopic view. It is the view where we feel that most things get done, and it's tempting to think that it's the most important view. However, you must have visibility in all three sections. All three views are forever connected. You can't dwell only in the area that is most comfortable for you, which far too many business owners (and folks in their careers) do. Just as a symphony needs the entire score of music to be moving, you can't pluck one note from the score and expect it to be profound. It has no meaning on its own without being part of the whole ecosystem, the entire experience.

Now that we know the individual items of the Trinity of Creativity (Concept, Idea, and Execution), the question becomes, How can we use this to enhance creativity?

Let's use an example to go along with the work you're doing. Let's pretend you own a pizza restaurant and work to identify all three of the pieces of the Trinity.

The Concept could be something like *sustenance* or *nourishment*. For this example, we will pick sustenance. Remember, this is the highest-level view of your product or service.

If the Concept is *sustenance*, the Idea would be something like *food* or, if you are a healthy pizza restaurant, *low-fat food* or *gluten-free food*. Let's go with *food* for now.

For the last piece of the Trinity, the Execution could be something like a *medium garlic meat superfan pizza that features sausage, pepperoni, meatballs, bell pepper, onion, and tomato-basil sauce, finished with a cheesy stuffed crust*. It's the specific laser-focused Execution that follows the Concept and the Idea.

LET'S MAKE CREATIVITY HAPPEN

Now that we understand the Trinity of Creativity, let's start to make creativity happen! We're not going to wait around for inspiration to strike; we're going to create actively.

Let's start by getting personal. Look at what you have written down and circled. The Trinity will enable you to develop new products creatively, innovate in new ways, and solve problems. It can be used for anything that plagues your business or career as a reliable formula to spark creativity.

Now let's dive deeper into what you wrote down for the Execution. We start with the Execution because that is the most finite adjustment we can make, subtle yet effective. Any adjustments at the Execution level give us subtle shades of new creative ideas where we need to start before bringing in the bigger guns of the Idea and the Execution, where changes become more pronounced.

Stare at what you have written for the Execution long and hard. Are alternatives popping into your head? That's creativity at work. Let your mind consider the variations and alternatives that pop up as you stare at what you have written without letting self-doubt creep in. Don't let ugly thoughts such as self-consciousness and worrying about what others may think stop you from writing down every single idea that pops into your head. Don't overthink but quickly consider what else comes to mind as variations on or alternatives to your Execution and write them down.

What you are doing here is coming up with subtle variations and alternatives that are based on your existing Execution. These subtle changes in the Execution offer you the seedlings of potential new creative products or even new directions in your career. The very act of focusing on your Execution and allowing your mind to come up with alternative variations is creativity beginning to work. Don't block it. You're not waiting for inspiration to strike. You are making it happen. While you are proposing alternatives to and variations on your Execution, you are activating the primordial mind that once championed creativity above all.

But you can't stop there!

Next, let's look at the Idea. Any tweaks here yield grander adjustments in creativity. Follow the familiar pattern of looking at the Idea you wrote down, letting your mind wander, and writing down any alternatives or variations that pop into your head. Again, don't think too much; just explore what ideas pop up for you. There is no wrong answer and no pressure.

Finally, let's do the same thing with the Concept of your business or career. Tweaks here will yield significant changes. Take a look at what you have written down and come up with one or two alternatives that are related to your Concept. Write them down so that you can generate options and allow creativity to take hold.

■   ■   ■

THE WORK WE JUST did enabled the creative mind to shut out the analytical mind so that it could actively practice *doing* creativity. In that creativity, innovation, new products, or different services will be revealed.

How?

By *identifying the Execution*, you should creatively enable:

- Slight variations on your product, service, or career goal

- Slight changes in the meaning of your product or service to you and the customer

- Subtle changes in how the product, service, or the career goal works

By *identifying the Idea*, you should creatively enable:

- Significant variations on new innovative products or services to take to market

- Considerable improvement opportunities

- A distinct and refreshed approach to existing problems

By *identifying the Concept*, you should creatively enable:

- Radical changes to your product, service, or career

- Extraordinary departures from your current path

- Major momentous shifts in your completely new and
  refined product, service, or career

Writing out your Trinity of Creativity may save your business, make your foundation stronger, or even launch you into profitability levels you've never seen before. It also may make your career great again. Each time you're stuck, no matter what the issue, complete this exercise. Each time you are frustrated by lack of promotion or advancement, use the Trinity. Heck, why not use it every quarter to keep fresh and nimble?

The work you do with the Trinity can be a way for you to look back and see how far you have come. Also, you can run the Trinity as a group, allowing your coworkers or staff to come up with different responses for each step of the Concept, Idea, and Execution. I use this exercise almost daily because it's so powerful in its ability to keep up with change and keep you fresh and relevant. And it's also one of my most popular requested workshops because its powerful process allows for endless creativity to be generated by anyone.

WHY THE CREATOR MINDSET AND WHY NOW?

Creativity is a monetizable skill that relies on an understanding of human nature to realize its full potential.

CHAPTER 5

The Brain and Heart on a Collision Course of Prosperity

brain + heart

T HE DEFINING FACTOR of the next generation in business will be established by companies and employees who learn how to balance the power of creativity with the relentless quest for the analytical. Above all else, this is the plain and simple truth of the arrival of the twenty-first-century creative economy: companies that are able to embrace a new way of thinking creatively will thrive, and those stuck in the analytical past will die. This movement is at its historical apogee, and adjusting accordingly has never been more important. As the global economy becomes more fluid and technology advances at breakneck speeds, this is the time to invest in joining the heart and the mind—the creative and the analytical—in ways that will increase value and make your product or service relevant in the new economy.

That all starts within us. As we learned in earlier chapters in this book, we have been bestowed with one of the most amazing devices the world has ever seen, and it's not something that we can go out and buy. It comes part and parcel with each human being on earth. It's the human brain. It has the most incredible ability to allow our actions and thoughts to become truly balanced and harmonious; we just have to relearn how to do it. We are all born with an innate ability to balance both the creative mind and the analytical mind to achieve what we are all capable of, yet most of us have not even begun to scratch the surface of our capabilities. Like an iceberg where you can see only a small tip above the water, our potential has been shrunk to a representation of our analytical only selves. It's time to show what is beneath the surface—the creative side—and reveal our whole selves to make our businesses and the world a better place.

Let's talk anatomically for a second to understand how creativity works. The mind is separated into two divisions. The left hemisphere deals mostly with issues of the analytical, including numbers, charts, measurements, and precision. The right hemisphere mostly deals with the realm of creativity, including music, questioning, dreaming, and envisioning. There is some crossover between the two divisions, but still you must choose carefully and work hard to make a harmonious balance. When operating in this balance, the human mind is the best computer ever. Its potential is truly limitless. Sadly, though, most of us do not use our thinking potential in full balance. Instead, we've built up the analytical side so much that we've disabled The Creator Mindset from the start. This can be fixed, but first we need to understand the errors that got us here:

1. *We have forgotten how to use the creative side of the brain to solve problems.* We are out of touch with what

we were in touch with when we were children: the ability to solve problems creatively before any other skill set emerged. Almost like a memory that has become fragmented as we age, creativity has become foggy as we have grown older. As a result, creative solutions we had when younger seem foreign to us because we have forgotten how to use these innate creative tools. We must remember that these creative tools are as basic to the human experience as breathing air and eating food.

2. *We have learned to turn down the volume on the creative side of our thinking process.* We aren't listening to ourselves even though our brains are forever trying. Have you ever told yourself lies such as "It's just a midlife crisis," "This is not reasonable," "No one would ever go for that," "That's not mature," and "This idea is too far-fetched"? Most of us have, and in doing so we have become our own worst enemy. We are full of self-doubt that we need to conquer (we'll talk about this in Chapter 15).

Our schooling is partially to blame for the dominance of the analytical mindset. We tend to like things we can see, things that can be expressed in numbers. Don't fall for that fallacy. The fact that something can be quantified doesn't mean that we have captured a sense of what it is. It is at best only part of the story. At worst, quantifying something will only assign a number or measurement that is meaningless while ignoring a host of wealth that is to be found in the creative view, which unlocks powerful emotional intelligence. More on this in a bit.

Our workplace is also partially to blame for the buildup of the analytical mindset. We think with spreadsheets and charts and reports and profit and loss statements as the guiding light.

We think that someone needs to show up in person and sit at a desk; because we can "see" that someone is working, we deduce that that person must be working. The business world has taught us to see these analytical things as the bible of our business while ignoring the emotional intelligence and soft skills that truly makes a difference in a product, service, or career. It is out of creativity that we strengthen and grow our emotional intelligence, and from that emotional intelligence we develop a sense of empathy, understanding, fairness, and connection to a greater cause. Using this newfound emotional intelligence in all aspects of your business from hiring to strategy will yield a profound shift in balance from the analytical to the creative.

Although there are many things to blame for the loss of creativity today, ultimately we are the ones to blame for this departure from creativity. We stopped listening to what we know we need to listen to. We see empathy as weakness in business. We see passion as being too assertive or aggressive in business. Women who speak up are called "bossy" or worse. Men who are assertive are seen as "aggressive" or worse. We see kindness as superfluous and redundant for the bottom line. Perhaps the saddest part is that whenever thoughts come up that really excite us or really get us thinking differently, we talk negatively about them and put them under lock and key. The Creator Mindset is trying to speak to us to show us a better path—a path of possibility— yet we shut it down.

It's because of this ignoring, forgetting, and putting down of the creative memory that our brains develop a highly unbalanced physical structure. Without operating both sides of our brains together, we will never be able to work to our fullest potential and instead get stuck wondering why we are not fulfilled.

Not balancing analytics with creativity is one of the reasons people are so unhappy all around the globe. We find ourselves always searching for that next "something": a new diet, exercise routine, or wardrobe. We're searching for something externally and ignoring the fact that the true path to success lies within each and every one of us from birth. We were born with it; we just need to learn how to operate it all over again.

I'd like for you to do another exercise. Start by thinking of something a bit differently than you are used to doing. Take the top right corner of this page and fold it in. Take the tip of the page and fold it back so that it makes a little triangle where the page number is. It should only be an inch or so—not too big. Now look at the page very carefully. The folded tip that you just made represents The Creator Mindset. It's tiny and is drowned out by the rest of the page. It even looks like a minor anecdote, a dog-eared page in a bunch of pages in a book. Now look at the rest of the page, the part that is not folded. That represents the analytical bandwidth that you have developed in your lifetime. It doesn't look too proportional, does it? It is a bit out of whack. The analytical is almost the entire page, whereas the creative is just a small corner on the page. Taking a look at this visual should give you an immediate impression of what is actually going on biologically. But the good news is that there is hope because the dog-eared portion of the page is still part of the page—they are one and the same. The fabric of the creative and that of the analytical are forever two sides of the same coin, or in this case two parts of the same page. They are grafted from one sheet of paper, as you can see in the triangle you have made. Just as easily, you can lift the little dog-ear you made and make a bigger triangle across the page. You can do exactly the same thing when it comes to your Creator Mindset. But for right now, I would like for you to rip out this tiny triangle and keep it somewhere where you can see it. Tape it to your computer monitor or put it by your nightstand. Each time you are about to think with the analytical mind only, it will be there to serve as a reminder to think with your whole potential instead.

■   ■   ■

SCIENTISTS HAVE BEEN WORKING on what they call artificial intelligence in computers since the dawn of computing.[1] It seems that technology is meant to replicate human behavior at all costs. The scientists want to create something that looks human, thinks like a human, and even talks like a human. Some of their results have been impressive, but only when it comes to analytical processing. Sure, a computer can process far more numbers than any human can. Its ability to be analytical is second to none. Computers can look for patterns in numbers, sequences in numbers, and the organization of numbers far better than we humans can.[2] But as amazing as the progress of computers has been, what is interesting to me is what a computer is not good at doing.

A computer is not good at replicating the creative side of the brain—at all. It struggles to deal with the creative side in the way that humans do without thinking about it. In fact, even at our turned-down volume of creativity, a computer still isn't a match. Creative attributes such as empathy, understanding, hope, aspiration, sympathy, passion, and creativity among many, many others define the human experience, and they are proving very difficult for computers to duplicate.

Scientists have started working on ways to make AI seem more "human."[3,4] They have tried to synthesize attributes of the creative mind such as forethought, concentration, kindness, justice, and love with little success. These attributes are part and parcel of the experience of being human. This is who we are. It's what gives our lives meaning.

That's why creativity is so important. It's got a finger on the nerve of what really matters to us humans. Using what really matters in your everyday business will build a powerful approach to an ever-changing marketplace. Whereas analytics and technology change from day to day, the principles of The Creator Mindset are forever fixed as the building blocks of who we are. That's what makes The Creator Mindset so important in all that you do: creativity will always allow one person to connect with another in meaningful ways. Imagine how powerful that can be for your business: staff member to staff member, business to business, business to customer, customer to customer. The number of tools at your disposal while you are thinking analytically is finite, numbered, limited, but the number of tools at your disposal while you are thinking creatively is endless.

To encourage creativity in any organization, we need to understand how human attributes work. We can learn more about this with another activity. This time, I want you to take a pen and write down in the margin what is the most important thing to you right now in your business or career. What do you really need or treasure? What is the most important thing to you right at this minute? There is no right answer, but your response needs to be deeply personal and reflective of where you are right now. Not tomorrow, not in 10 years, but where you are right this minute. Trust me, this will change throughout your life and sometimes even throughout your day.

Now I want you to take whatever you have written down and begin to look at it with The Creator Mindset. Can money being important to you right now actually mean that security is important? What about access to a particular market? Does that really mean that empathy with your niche is paramount? Really think about your answer and find the creative human element that brings new opportunity and defines things in a way that is accessible to your innate emotional intelligence. It is the key that unlocks the door, because when we stop to define our lives only in the analytical mindset and start to examine them with The Creator Mindset, we begin to use the emotional intelligence part of our brain. As a result, we activate a holistic solution that is not derived from the outdated theories of yesterday. Our mind will prepare a custom solution for a problem, but it cannot do that if we don't change the paradigm of how we think. Turn up the volume now on that part of your brain. Do it while analyzing a particular issue with your business. Force yourself to see it differently. It is trying to tell you what to do and suggest a solution. Don't be afraid of the emotional intelligence it generates. It will become more and more familiar to you as you remember its power. It will enable you to connect with your staff and your customers. It will enable you to grow in ways you have never imagined. It will be the key factor in embracing creativity in all you do and will enable you to be relevant in the new creative economy. Turn the volume up right now. What is it saying?

6

harriette

When Nothing Else Works, Creativity Will

I T WAS A dark and stormy night roughly 100,000 years ago during the last ice age. Harriette, an early human, ran into her cave. She was not having a good day. Sopping wet from the storm, she was further pummeled by pounding rain moving sideways into her cave. It was miserable. She then heard footsteps getting louder and louder from just outside the cave. "Oh, damn," she thought. "What now?" Her shelter was primitive at best—just an opening in an outcropping of rocks—but it was the best she could do. She had some basic tools but nothing we would consider as being of any real utility today. She looked down and noticed the floor begin to rise as a flood beckoned. She heard the footsteps get louder and louder. She looked down at her meager tools. They were now floating. A sharp snap was heard just outside her shelter. It was a saber-toothed cat[1] standing four feet high at its shoulders and eight and half feet long. It weighed almost 600 pounds, had 13-inch fangs, and had an appetite for early humans.

Hunting season was on for these early animals 100,000 years ago. They had dominion over the entire globe. They were able to hunt with impunity and take what they wanted. They didn't differentiate between humans and other animals. It was a violent world where the average early human didn't see his or her thirtieth birthday,[2] in large part because these beasts were such good killing machines. To say that the Earth was a slaughter ground is an understatement. Early humans like Harriette needed something to help them stay alive. They were outmatched by these animals in every way. The animals were faster and larger, and their senses were better. They were ferocious in every conceivable way. Only one thing stood between death and survival for those early humans: *creativity*.

Harriette was face-to-face with imminent death. The beast was now at her doorstep. Yet Harriette remained eerily calm. Just yesterday a similar beast had attacked and hauled off two other humans from her village. With the screams of her kinfolk echoing in her head, she stopped and composed herself. She had a creative idea, the world's first for a human. She looked down at her floating tools and saw an arrowhead she had crafted to collect berries from jagged bushes. She had never seen that tool as anything but a berry picker. Then she saw a large branch from a tree. She had never seen a branch as anything other than a branch. But with the power of creativity she put the two together. At the most perilous time, an idea was sparked, and all of a sudden there was a slight chance she could stave off the beast. In a few quick terrifying moments while avoiding the fangs of the attacking animal, she fastened the arrowhead to the end of the stick. And a new tool was created.

Creativity saved Harriette's life, and creativity was born out of necessity. It's ingrained in our very DNA as an attribute of humanity that is necessary for survival.[3] Without creativity we wouldn't be alive today. The Earth was filled with animals far stronger, far bigger, and far more violent than humans. We would not have made it had it not been for creativity. This is not frivolous stuff. This is a matter of living or dying. Creativity is the very substance of life.

Over and over the story remains much the same. There is some adversity. Creativity wins. Adversity is overcome through the principles of human ingenuity that manifests itself time and time again as creativity. We learned which plants to eat. We learned how to build the best shelters. We learned how to make jugs to carry water a long distance. We learned how to fish. We learned how to hunt. We learned how to build a bridge over water to get to the other side. Airplanes, robots to Mars, and so on and so forth—all creative efforts.

All the largest developments in our history came from the power of the idea. Someone much like Harriette came up with some idea at some point and solved some problem. Let's get to the moon. How? No one has ever gotten to the moon! It is time to get creative. Creativity can solve problems that are unsolvable if we look only to the current darling of human thinking: the analytical rubric. Historical events are often wrongly attributed to who won this or that war or who conquered whom. That is missing the point because creativity is—no matter how you use it, from warfare to welfare—the glue that binds all human accomplishments.

But creativity comes with a pretty strong side effect, and it happens to be a wonderful altruistic side effect. Creativity comes with a contiguous energy that allows any idea to spread. As deeply as creativity is ingrained in us, so is its side effect. Harriette ran back to her village immediately after she thwarted the attack to share her new tool. Jonas Salk, who invented the polio vaccine, immediately rushed to push it out to the world for free. It was too important not to share.[4] The guys who started Tesla shared with their friends and families each milestone of their new development so that they too could feel the rush of the electric car. There were lines to ride their prototype around the parking lot![5] Thinking with a Creator Mindset allows the idea to spread far and wide, and there is a contagious energy that unites everybody with the championing of the idea. It crosses class, ethnic, and socioeconomic boundaries. It is a sheer joy that emanates from the deepest recesses of our innate altruistic vision of the world. No one really gets excited by seeing an analytical spreadsheet of numbers endlessly hanging off the bottom of a report or another analytical PowerPoint presentation. But creativity captures everyone's imagination each and every time.

Today it is not enough to just survive. We look to thrive— and so we should. We want to grow our businesses. We want to do more faster, better, and more efficiently. We want to leave the world a better place for our children and their children. Here in its most basic form is the stuff of life: creativity. What better tool of the human condition can we possibly use to improve our standing in life than creativity?

Now that we have established how creativity is ingrained in our experience as humans, imagine how harnessing it in your business or career will grow it, shape it, make it relevant, and make it successful. You are tapping into a nerve that makes us who we are. It is the very stuff that makes us tick. If you are able to use and harness creativity in your business, you have a direct path into our primordial minds and our emotions. You have a one-way ticket to a nerve center full of emotion designed to get someone to react to what you are doing.

Apple knew this when it designed beautiful-looking yet fully functional technology. They designed more than a computer. They designed an iconic technology experience. Tesla knew it too. Sure, they designed a nice car, but more impressive is the fact that the car became a lifestyle item that shouts a person's values and personality to the world. This is primordial creativity at work.

Connecting to who we are and what we want at the most intimate level allows products and services that derive from The Creator Mindset to thrive in a way an analytical approach can never accomplish. Creativity works because it connects us to long-lost ancestral needs, needs that you can position your company or career to take advantage of.

Positioning your company or career to take advantage of the intimate connection creativity gives us is nothing to have compunctions about. We often vilify corporations by saying that they are taking advantage of us by selling us stuff we don't need, but when this is looked at creatively, it is not true. Corporations are beholden to us, and we vote with what we buy. None of these companies would be in business if we didn't consume their products. Companies have made our basic survival so easy. Why? Because we *want* them to.

Our environment today is far removed from the daily fight to survive our ancestors had to deal with—and that's all thanks to creativity.

You see, in a way creativity *reminds* us of our function as human beings. It reminds us of what our ancestors endured, and it drives us closer and closer to our real selves. It puts us back in touch with the pure essence of our humanity, which is the fact that we were filled with creativity designed to solve problems and triumph over adversity on an intimate level.

Today we need it more than ever. We need it because we no longer rely on fight or flight from this or that beast. We are no longer afraid for our lives from one moment to another. Adrenaline and dopamine are still active inside us to guard against primordial death, but they are triggered only by things such as riding roller coasters and solving crossword puzzles.[6] That's how far we have come. We need to stimulate the basic human functions that used to entail far more significant consequences in order to feel alive today. Commoditizing creativity meets that need and is nothing to be ashamed of or bashful about. Free enterprise is the heartbeat of the global economy because it is what is needed most to connect us to our real selves.

7

the flu

A World That Can Be, Not a World That Is

A FEW YEARS BACK I caught a bad cold and the doctor prescribed a few medications and sent me on my way. I was hopeful when I arrived at the pharmacy to pick up my meds, but all hope was dashed when I discovered that the meds she'd prescribed did nothing for the cause of my cold; they only treated the symptoms. A cough medicine and a nasal decongestant—that was it. Luckily, I felt better quickly, but one thought has stayed with me: there was a direct parallel between business and cold symptoms. Most business treat symptoms, not the root cause of the problem.[1] Although there are many in medicine who are working bravely to solve the root problem of countless diseases, it seems not many of us are looking to solve the root cause of problems in our businesses or even in ourselves.

It's not surprising to me that issues are not being fixed because the analytical mindset has limited potential to fix problems.

It seems that we rely on the same old antiquated policies of managing the symptoms of problems in business instead of fixing the root causes of those problems. Fixing those issues takes imagination, a construct of creativity, and we must relearn how to use it.

I'd like you to do another exercise. Imagine a world that is not bound by limitation, a world that is not bound by constraints or physical barriers. Right now, on these very pages, I will reveal to you a secret that is not really a secret, though we can call it one if we want to. This secret is beautiful in its simplicity and elegant in its candor. Like everything else in this book, it relies on reawakening what you already know and are able to use just by willing it. Are you ready?

Close your eyes and take a deep breath. Now open your eyes and imagine a world that can be shaped by any idea that you have simply because you declare it. But as you declare the idea, say it with positivity, not negativity. Creativity is the playground of the positive thinker. Negativity is the playground of the irrelevant: the company or career that has been, the product or service that no one wants anymore. Positivity is the fertile ground of creativity, and it is a key ingredient in enabling innovation in The Creator Mindset. The secret is the power of positivity.

Imagination, as you used it in the last paragraph, depends on mastery of the language of positivity. That language is a tool in The Creator Mindset that allows you to focus on the positive outcome of what happens even if the outcome is not what you have envisioned.

It's a shift in mentality that allows the creative side of the brain to see "yes" while the analytical side is screaming "no." It's a tool to lower the volume on the "no" so that you can hear more "yes." Its focus is the very words you use to describe the effect that you want. Instead of saying "this doesn't work," say "this is different from what I thought." Instead of saying "this is terrible," say "this is unexpected." It's a slight shift but an important one because there is a strong cause-and-effect process in The Creator Mindset that allows the language of permission to guide you to places that you were unaware that you needed to go. In other words, while we spend so much of our time trying to control (analytical) the narrative of our businesses or our careers, allowing input to differ from your predetermined outcome (creative) just might spark that new idea.

We spend so much time trying to control outcomes that we leave little time for something new and fresh to happen. That new idea cannot spark if you kill it before it's born with pessimism, negativity, and ego. A study in *Psychology Today* said that 80 percent of our daily thoughts are negative thoughts.[2] Holy cow! Eighty percent? That made everything click for me. I now understand that analytically, it's just so easy to say "no," and "no" tends to squash any creative endeavor before it begins. Words like *can't* or *won't* and *not* do the same thing. Instead, start using words that encourage creativity such as *maybe* and *let's see where this goes* and even *yes* to allow more creative ideas to be generated.

Where are we at today? Most businesses envision a world that is. It is full of problems, limitations, caps, boundaries, and other things that bar you from success. This is the one and only view of the world that is pushed by the analytical mindset. But I am here to argue that it is useless. Why view something in a rubric that gives you limited and uncreative options bound by past pessimism and tried-and-true solutions that are irrelevant today? Moreover, why view things the way everyone else does? You are an individual, and your business or profession is an extension of that individuality. It's what gives you your identity, your edge, your brand.

The Creator Mindset thrives when it is partnered with positivity. At its heart lies the simplicity of looking at the glass as being half-full. There is a magical transformation that occurs when you allow yourself to think about problems creatively. Allowing creativity to make a plan full of optimism breeds options to overcome adversity, and let's face it, when a business challenge emerges, all we want are options for overcoming that challenge. To allow creativity to activate fully, though, we must embrace the language of positivity as we enact The Creator Mindset. This positivity sometimes is difficult to conjure, but it is a critical element in the full breadth of executing The Creator Mindset.

I can imagine that you may be feeling a bit queasy about this. I mean, having excessive inventory piling up instead of going out the door will bring up many feelings, most of them negative. Having to buy new and expensive machines to fill an order may bring up similar feelings. These negative feelings, such as frustration, annoyance, dread, and maybe even anger, along with any other negative feelings, are not constructive or actionable. They are destructive.

When you are angry, you tend to make decisions that are not thought out, not prepared, not premeditated. Instead, you tend to act out in anger with swiftness and severity and without considering the options you so badly need. Instead of anger, positivity will bring up options. It will create a road map to emerge from the situation in which you currently find yourself. It will move you away from impulse, and positivity will build an actionable plan.

How will the language of positivity build an actionable plan? Let's take a look at an excessive inventory issue as an example. The immediate thought here probably will be negative. Excessive inventory sucks no matter how you look at it. I'm not naïve. I get it. It sparks questions that are hard to answer, such as What is contributing to this issue? Is it lack of effective sales? Did we overorder? Are things not moving in a certain market in which we thought they would move? Almost inevitably, these questions lead to someone to blame or punish. But if you shift to The Creator Mindset, these issues turn into potential catalysts for solutions that will be obvious only if you view the problems positively. I know that this may seem counterintuitive, but it works. I've seen it work, and it will work for you. You can move mountains by approaching problems with the language of positivity.

Let's try looking at this problem of inventory with The Creator Mindset by viewing what is working instead of focusing on analytical negativity. Ask yourself these two questions:

1. How can we look at this problem positively to allow options to seep into our consciousness?

2. How can we look at this problem to allow ideas to come up without relying on the old way of viewing it?

Think of any issue you have in your business today and apply these two questions. When you think creatively about problems in your business or profession, you open up options that can touch different areas and lead to effectiveness for not just the problem you are working on but for other problems as well: both the symptom and the root cause. My example here is vague on purpose. I want you to think of whatever specific issue you are encountering and see the parallels. If you take a creative view of the stuff piling up at the warehouse, ask if it perhaps is time to cut your losses and clear out stuff that isn't moving. Sometimes things are blessings in disguise. Maybe this will lead to a clearing out that will allow you to take on the next order more efficiently. Maybe the market is telling you something about your product. If that is the case, what? Are you listening? Have you been listening, and have you listened lately? Perhaps this is the time to talk to customers and see what their perception is. When was the last time you hit the road and really talked to your customers? Maybe this is the time to engage with your team members to see what their perception is.

Rarely is a problem an island in a business. It usually is tied to a couple of different things that work in concert to bring either success or failure. I am not privy to your particular problem, and these suggestions are all generic. But they are based on The Creator Mindset and rooted in the two questions we just discussed. You know far more than I do about your issues and their history in your company. Now it is time for you to declare that looking at issues with the old view is no longer relevant. Getting creative about solving problems positively will allow you to attack the core issue, not just the symptoms.

But why are we so predisposed to the negative side of life? Why is it so much easier to look at the glass as being half empty? Why is it in our human nature to react negatively so easily? Why are we humans not easily disposed to positivity as a matter of course? The human condition is designed to survive and not do what we are doing today. We are doing far more than just surviving; we're thriving.

Our experience as humans has changed drastically in just the past 50 years, and tens of thousands of years of evolution are still catching up to the current situation. Anger used to give us the boost of this or that hormone to have the strength to defeat the attacking beast the way Harriette did in Chapter 6. But today that anger produces the same hormone it did for our ancestors while we stare at boxes piling up in a warehouse. Do you see how terribly misplaced this reaction is for dealing with the problem in front of us? Without the language of positivity to absorb our perspective in a Creator Mindset, we are simply following along like everyone else, forever stuck in the dogma of our past. We need to retrain our minds to see things a different way.

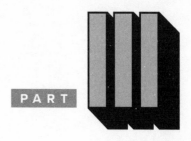

PART III

USING THE CREATOR MINDSET

The success of implementing The Creator Mindset relies on detailed principles that we will discuss in the following chapters. Some principles may initially feel counterintuitive, yet each is a tool that must be mastered to achieve creative success.

CHAPTER **8**

Creativity's Unlikely Personality Traits

the coffee van

WHEN I WAS a kid, I worked for a coffee delivery service in Hollywood. On the surface this may seem like a glamorous job, but like most jobs that seem glamorous, it was anything but. Sure, there were trips to movie sets and television stages and I got to meet a celebrity or two on one of the coffee and doughnut drop-offs, but by and large it was nonglamorous delivery service work. There were the early mornings for starters, including the 4 a.m. doughnut pickups so they would be fresh for the 6 a.m. drop-offs. There was the endless washing of coffeepots with scouring pads and soap. It took me almost 10 years to like coffee again. The smell of those coffeepots would drive anyone to become a tea lover.

The silver lining was the fact that I had a great boss, a man named Jeff Chean. Great bosses make you stick around no matter how unglamorous or hard the work is. On top of being a great boss, Jeff would give me flyby quips, insights into the human condition. "Cheanisms" he called them. There were quips such as "the work you do is a service to others." I thought we were making coffee for a bunch of spoiled Hollywood people, but he made sure that the work we did was seen as a service to others. Jeff had other quips too, such as "Tuck in your shirt and comb your hair. No one wants to buy anything from a bum." He was largely right in those quick teachings. It was almost like a real-world business education executed in five-second snippets.

Jeff's knowledge was profound, and it helped me realize that there are three attributes of our personalities that are essential compared with all the others in overcoming problems creatively:

1. Humor

2. Empathy

3. Courage

These three personality traits are built into each and every one of us. Once we realize that, we must begin to use all three together and in combination to make sure that creativity can take hold and generate innovation in everything we do.

These are the elements I've found that spark creativity time and time again. Why? Because they inspire creativity and lead you to more innovation, wealth, and growth. Pretty awesome, isn't it?

We have to start learning how to use them for creativity. How do we do that? First, by taking a bit of time to look at each one of these attributes on its own.

CREATIVITY'S UNLIKELY PERSONALITY TRAITS

Humor

Many people believe that humor is not the stuff of serious, intellectual, studious, or successful types. But keeping yourself open to humor will make your effort in creativity all the more worthwhile because it offers an insight into the fallacy of thinking that we are in control of anything—which we are not. You see, humor represents a force that tells us—and others—that it is okay to fail. It's okay to be human. It's okay to get it wrong. The Creator Mindset depends on this permission to fail in order to get it right. Making mistakes is one of the key ingredients of innovation, as you will see in Chapter 11, where we look at 3M's Post-it Notes and other stories of mistakes that turned into amazing products or services.

Humor is also important because it allows us to relax a bit. It grants us permission to see the funny side of life. With humor, we can change the way we see problems in our businesses or our careers. Let's revisit our overloaded warehouse inventory problem from Chapter 7 as an example. If you're dealing with a situation in which you have too much inventory and nowhere for it to go and you react with anger, you will eliminate just about all creative solutions to the problem. But if you look at it with humor and perhaps say something like "Hey, look, we've got a lot of merch in here; maybe we should have the merch monster come and eat all this stuff up," you allow others to look at the situation a little more lightly and with humor. It might not be all that funny, but that's okay. We're simply using humor as a tool to cut loose a bit and spark a creative idea. After hearing that one silly remark, someone might say, "Actually, I've got an idea. What if we move the stuff to a storage place down the street called Monster Storage, which charges a dollar for the first month? We can then discount the inventory within that month and move it." And so a brilliant idea comes to life because you chose to look at the situation with humor.

Humor ultimately allows you to find a creative solution because it works in subtle and disarming ways. It is indeed the stuff of the studious and serious, because it creates opportunities to connect with the basic truth that we are not all that much in control all the time. And *that's* funny. Sometimes a bit of humor can go a long way toward humanizing problems and allowing creative solutions to unfold.

On top of it all, humor makes us more fun to be around, and at the end of the day, that's what it's all about. It makes us relatable. It makes us likable. It makes us connect with others. We spend so much of our time dedicating ourselves to our work, but what we really remember is not the assignment we completed or the deadline we met. What we tend to remember is the people we work with and, one hopes, their humor in tough situations.

Empathy

Empathy is the second critical tool in creativity's unlikely personality traits, and it's one of my favorites because it is so versatile.

Empathy comes in two forms when you look at it in the context of my process:

- *Internal empathy* is a result of looking at internal issues in your company or career with creativity.

- *External empathy* is a result of looking outside your company or career with creativity.

Internal Empathy

Internal empathy boils down to actually listening to your staff members and coworkers, listening to what is going on within your company so that you can relate. In the hallways, in the conference rooms, on the road trips, in meetings—really listening. Internal empathy is not what people say about your company or what your reputation is; internal empathy is the inner workings of your relationships and connections inside the company. When looked at through the lens of The Creator Mindset, internal empathy ultimately boils down to understanding that business transactions are about the customers, not about you. Empathy for the customers' needs is the essence of creativity because it allows you to satisfy those needs with your product or service at just the time when the customers need it the most.

Internal empathy is also the understanding that looking inside the company or your career and building meaningful relationships is a worthwhile goal. Why? Because in the rush to vilify an external concern such as the fact that the market is hard for sales right now or the boss doesn't want to promote you, it flips the tables. It puts the burden of responsibility on *you* to try to figure out your own destiny. What can you be doing better? How can you work better with others? What one thing can you do today, internally, to make your path brighter? These questions will help you shine a light on the power you hold in your life, career, and business.

My favorite case study of internal empathy involves a lawn care service company I did a keynote for a while back. They had a pretty sizable chunk of the market in a particular location but not much work elsewhere. The excuses for that ran deep until one day someone on the staff got creative and took the initiative to come up with a creative idea about how to win new business. Internal empathy led coworkers to get excited about the idea.

How? They started listening to one another, interacting, exploring together. Soon this idea led to exponential growth all because someone decided not to complain or blame others. Instead the company pushed a creative idea forward and made its business more successful.

External Empathy

External empathy comes about when you are looking at an issue outside of your business honestly, without pretense or judgment. It's about listing to what external factors are telling you. Not only that, it is about looking at external factors such as the competition—why that superstar was snatched away and hired by someone else or why someone else got a promotion and you didn't—as a source of learning, growing, and understanding, not judgment or negativity.

I cannot tell you how often when I am out speaking or consulting about The Creator Mindset, someone in the audience will ask me how to beat his or her competition. The story always boils down to their competitors driving the prices down in a race to the bottom. They wonder, How can I compete? They pass judgment. They are negative and critical. The answer almost always encompasses my concept of external empathy because I ask that person how much engagement he or she has with the competition. The answer usually comes back the same: None. Why should I talk to them? Why should I relate to them? They are my competition.

Then I ask the person if he or she has assessed the marketplace or his or her position within the company honestly by using external empathy, not just passing judgment at arm's length. Usually, we are so busy passing judgment on what we *think* the truth is that we do not empathize or relate to anyone else,

CREATIVITY'S UNLIKELY PERSONALITY TRAITS 67

especially our competition. When we pass judgment, we lose a creative advantage.

You see, it's actually imperative to relate to your competition because there is a valuable insight to gain. For example, look at the special way they market their product or service or perhaps their unusually decentralized office. You pass judgment by thinking, Everyone's working from home! How can they get anything done? Instead of looking at this with anger or frustration, try to be creative. Look at it with curiosity and try to learn. Ask yourself, What can I learn from this decentralized office? What are they gaining from having people work from home? What can I borrow from them so that I can improve my own standing or career? By doing that, you will find clues to help you improve your business or career to compete more effectively.

There is a world of creative wealth that can be had by studying these clues. It just takes the will to try.

External empathy is not about passing judgment on the competition. External empathy is instead a creative tool that allows you to look honestly at your career or company and assess it against external forces in an honest and fair way. There you will unlock opportunity.

Courage

Courage is one of the most difficult components of The Creator Mindset to master. You need courage to find out what you are doing wrong and try something new to fix it. It takes a lot of guts to look at yourself and recognize that there is room for improvement. It takes courage to look for things that we can improve on in both our careers and our companies. It takes courage to accept that there is a better way to do something. Then it takes heaps of courage to try something different, new, and creative.

Courage also involves the innate creativity that Harriette our ancestor in Chapter 6 had when she took a pointed stick and fought because there was no other choice. Today, courage deals with believing in yourself and knowing that your direction is the right direction to go in no matter how much things are stacked up against you. Sounds a lot like our ancestor's definition of courage, doesn't it? There may not be the data to support your gut feeling and the analytics may be pointing in another direction, but courage allows that creative instinct to point you where you need to go. And that is courageous.

When you are following The Creator Mindset, courage allows you to look for answers in places that seem off limits, places that may seem uncomfortable, places that may seem rife with fear. Because this creative courage I am talking about is the belief that creativity can conquer all, it is indeed worthwhile to try to conquer your fears.

I am certain that you are dealing with some issue right at this moment, perhaps even toying around with a solution. But you don't think it's good enough for whatever reason. Creative courage is the will to try that idea as a potential creative solution and believe in your ability to make that creative leap.

Courage is listening to creativity when analytics have mostly been the louder. It takes courage to listen to creativity *and* consider analytics as well. It takes courage to forge forth a path to unite your thinking, giving each and every problem 100 percent.

Using courage in The Creator Mindset is difficult. Because it involves looking within to see what we are doing wrong, it is just plain hard. We spend so much of our lives, both professional and personal, trying not to look at our flaws. Therefore, courage becomes one of the hardest tools to master. But like anything in life, sometimes the harder something is, the more worthwhile it is. As with running a marathon or completing an advanced degree, the fact that something is hard doesn't mean that we shouldn't do it. Perhaps it means that we should be doing more of it. The same thing is true when we look at courage deep within ourselves and recognize our flaws in order to make ourselves more creative.

■   ■   ■

HUMOR, EMPATHY, AND COURAGE are three unlikely personality traits of creativity that I find over and over are most successful. It turns out that these three traits are deeply useful in negotiating the often treacherous and ever-changing landscape of business today because they are universal. Putting them all together and being *actively conscious* of putting them together in your dealings with everyday problems will yield amazing and elevated creative results.

allen

On the Virtues of Listening

A FEW YEARS AGO, I ran an advertising agency for an eccentric owner we'll call Allen for the sake of this story. He had hired me specifically to run the agency and make sure that the company was profitable. I was given a leash as long as it could be, and it was my first time in charge. As long as revenue came in and Allen made a profit, he was happy. Allen had some very interesting quirks, including telling inappropriate stories with too much information at inappropriate times, all of which ended with him being the hero. But among all his quirks, the one that cost him the greatest amount of business was this: he talked far too much and listened far too little.

Much of our success is all about how we decide to spend and make the most of the precious resource of time. The Creator Mindset has some unique tools and skills that can be applied to time management and, of course, listening more and talking less, Both are key ingredients in allowing creativity to make a business or career far more effective—and for ensuring that you don't become like Allen.

Here are three proven and battle-hardened Creator Mindset methods to help you approach time management in a creative way:

1. Meetings

2. Microlistening

3. Shutting up

MEETINGS

A recent study of corporate America found that 67 percent of meetings are a complete waste of time.[1] Doesn't that sound crazy? Most meetings yield no results! What can we do about this, and how can we get better at managing our time creatively? First, we need to have a point at each and every meeting. The "why" factor of a meeting is important because it provides the framing to kick-start creativity. Sometimes we cannot control the length of meetings or even their frequency, but what we can always control is our approach. First and perhaps most important, don't be afraid to ask, "Why are we having this meeting?" It is the question in and of itself that sparks creativity as it helps the meeting become anchored in purpose. Second, if we can, we need to limit the time a meeting lasts. We cannot have meetings that drag on and on for no reason. Since most meetings yield only two or three minutes of productivity, why not limit the time of a meeting accordingly? Third, we need derivative action items: what can be done *today* as a result of the meeting to solve problems *now*. We need a take-away from that short meeting so that all the participants know what they need to do.

This is how creativity kicks in. As we challenge the why of the meeting and then institute a limitation on its time and finally an action plan, we set up a series of events that cascade into firing up creative solutions so that problems can be solved with a fresh perspective.

MICROLISTENING

Microlistening is essentially about *selective and limited listening*, meaning that you gather a limited audience when you are looking for opinions, advice, and/or feedback. When it comes to microlistening, we choose to accept only a few trusted sources to learn their opinion or get their feedback or advice. Microlistening is not listening to each and every person with some opinion on this or that.

This type of listening saves both time and money. Most people think that gathering research, testing a new product or service, or gaining opinions involves extensive research that sucks up both time and money, but that is not always the case. Sometimes it takes only a small sample size to come up with a profound insight. In a rush to gain feedback, testing results, or advice about the trajectory of our careers, sometimes we listen to far too many people. We overlisten when instead we should microlisten. Focusing on a small sample size can help you determine what is working and how to move forward.

I once worked for a brilliant chief marketing officer of a Fortune 500 company. No matter how much money was spent on testing the effectiveness of the advertising, public relations, or marketing he was putting out, he had an inexpensive yardstick by which he measured the effectiveness of any new initiative. He microlistened. He would simply ask carefully selected and trusted friends and colleges their opinion, and more often than not those opinions were right. He asked a broad enough group for their opinions but did not expand it to hundreds of people. He kept it small. Then he listened. Sure, the sample size was small and analytically it's easy to scoff at this idea, but it was brilliantly, creatively effective. Start using microlistening with trusted associates to gain valuable feedback, advice, and opinions today.

SHUTTING UP

Our urge to talk comes from a deeply seated belief that we want some vindication of our thoughts.[2] It's our egos yearning to express some point that we think is valuable. But when it is looked at creatively, something incredible begins to emerge about our urge to talk. It's actually counterintuitive, but go with me here: the ability to be heard goes up exponentially the less you talk. Isn't that amazing?

Basically, the less you talk and the more you think about what you want to say, the more you increase your chances of being heard. The more you shut up, the more you increase your chances of *hearing* something that is profound and worthwhile and incredibly valuable.

It's a wonderful thing that you can enact today as part of your embrace of The Creator Mindset. Resist the urge to chime in thoughtlessly just to fill time and really think about what you want to say. Keep your ears open. Then measure each word with great care and don't waste your chance to say what you mean.

The Creator Mindset looks at listening as one of the essential human traits that brought about modernity. In the past, our lives depended on listening to what people were saying to ensure survival. We needed to listen to stories about not eating this or that berry to avoid getting poisoned. We needed to listen to find out the best passage route over the mountains to avoid getting stuck in the cold of winter. We needed to listen to Harriette from Chapter 6 to discover a self-defense method to fight the beast looking to kill us. Yet something mysterious has happened over time. We have stopped listening.

The modern mind has given listening a bad name.[3] We think that people have ulterior motives and that listening to them would give us a skewed view of the facts or even lies. Thus, we would succumb to some kind of manipulation just by listening to one another. Perhaps that is why we talk so much and listen so little: we are afraid of being manipulated. Therefore, we try to control the situation by talking nonstop.

But the fear of being manipulated by listening to what someone else is saying is cutting short any opportunity to learn creatively. When we listen, a host of learning can occur. From the details of the way someone views a situation all the way to the spirit of what someone is trying to say nonverbally, there are infinite lessons to be learned.

Of course, this is not to say that you should take everything someone says at face value, but the creative wealth you gain by listening far outweighs any disadvantage.

■   ■   ■

OUR ABILITY TO MANAGE our time has taken on huge significance. It is a rightful cause. Time is more valuable than anything else, and figuring out how to make the best use of it is crucial when it comes to The Creator Mindset. Time is the one thing that once gone, we can never get back. Listening more carefully and talking less can yield amazing results the first time you try it, so start listening more effectively today.

The Importance of the Little Victory

sloppy burger

O NE OF MY earliest memories involves finding a parking spot. I know this was not a matter of great substance, but it was a little victory and it set up a lifetime of learning to appreciate the value of little victories. After finding the parking spot, I took one of those quarter rides outside a supermarket, and it was amazing fun. The parking spot had nothing to do with the ride, but it forever cemented a relationship between little victories and the potential for huge opportunities they offer.

You see, big victories mean nothing unless we stop to recognize the little victories that got us there along the way. It is all the little victories that add up to the whole, and sometimes that whole takes us to unexpected places with unexpected victories. Don't get where I'm going with this? Let's use a car trip as an example.

If your big goal is to get to Bashanville, USA, and you are in Seguraville, USA, which is 150 miles away, most people would plot the most direct path to get there because getting there is the big victory. But when you actually get on the highway for the big trip to Bashanville, you discover that there has been some construction work and you have to get off the main road and onto a side road. You may be tempted to look at this as a setback from your big victory of arriving at Bashanville. But when you look at it creatively, this is anything but a setback because off this side road, you stop and have an unexpected amazing burger at a roadside joint. This is a little victory that makes the big goal worthwhile. No matter what, the little victories along the way have the potential to be more interesting, more meaningful, and more rewarding than the big victory in the end. Sometimes you arrive at your final destination and sometimes you don't, but that doesn't take away the value of the little victories along the way.

Businesses and careers are no different.

Creatively, a little victory is a benchmark that you can use to allow more and more little victories to occur even if those victories take you to unexpected places. Here's what I mean: Perhaps your dream is to open a cupcake bakery on Main Street, and so you get excited about the idea. That is a little victory. You test your cupcake recipe on selected trusted associates who tell you it is the best cupcake ever. That is a little victory. Then you decide to incorporate your cupcake business by registering as an LLC. That is a little victory. When you are waiting to file the LLC, you meet someone in the waiting room who tells you he has a friend who is a chef and she would love your cupcakes. That is a little victory. You meet this chef friend, and she decides to buy your full supply of cupcakes. That too is a little victory.

At this point you may say, "Nir, that takes us away from our dream of opening a cupcake bakery on Main Street. We cannot veer away from our dream! That is the big victory; that is the main goal. If the chef buys all our cupcakes, the dream of opening up a cupcake bakery on Main Street is shattered." Well, that is true only if you look at it from the analytical mindset. The analytical mindset will accept nothing but the total fulfillment of the predetermined and very specific result (in this case opening a brick-and-mortar Main Street retail cupcake establishment).

But when you look at little victories from a Creator Mindset, the definition of your goals takes on a far more fluid and interesting aspect. Something very profound begins to occur. You begin to recognize that little victories can and will be a series of tangential yet connected occurrences that are just as important as the fulfillment of the predetermined result, which in this case was opening a brick-and-mortar cupcake shop on Main Street. I would argue that the creative occurrence of the little victories is far more important than the predetermined result—far more important.

Why?

When we look at things creatively, we allow ourselves to open up to the reality of what the little victories may be telling us. Perhaps opening a brick-and-mortar store on Main Street wasn't really the end goal after all, and allowing creativity to shape your destiny just might lead to a better product or service. You can see this in a career path or a company's path. When we look at little victories creatively, we do not limit our potential to what we have predetermined as the only measure of success. *We instead lift all barriers and limitations so that success can become boundless.*

I am not suggesting that we abandon a predetermined result. After all, we can always open a brick-and-mortar cupcake shop on Main Street at some point later. There are plenty of businesses and careers that follow a completely linear path. A occurs, then B, followed by C and then D, and so on. That's okay, but far more careers and companies take a different route. What I am suggesting is that it's okay for the path—for the little victories—to jump around out of order. Embracing the disorder and finding meaning in it is a little victory of creativity.

The truth is that most people would get discouraged at the first sign of a problem or even a perceived problem, of a detour or a nonlinear path to the predetermined result they hold so dear. But that's all right because sometimes a detour can become more richly rewarding than the predetermined result.

Remember our roadside burger example? There was once an entrepreneur whose main goal—his big victory—was to sell as many ice cream machines as humanly possible to as many people as possible. But soon his business was faltering. He needed to get creative. Should he find a different machine to sell? Should he find a new market? He kept thinking of short-term analytical solutions that would put a Band-Aid on the problem. But one day while he was delivering a bunch of ice cream machines to a southern California restaurant, he stumbled upon the best burger he'd ever had—with a line of people out the door who seemed to agree. He decided then and there to listen to what the little victory was telling him: Maybe his job was not to keep selling ice cream machines. Maybe, just maybe, it was telling him to get into the restaurant business with the goal of making the best burgers possible. That is creativity. His little victories ended up being a much bigger victory than selling ice cream machines. His name was Ray Croc, and his restaurant is now what we all know as McDonald's.[1]

Although this may not be the most traditional story of little victories adding up, it proves an important point: your goals can and probably will change as a result of your little victories along the way. Ray Croc allowed his little victories to guide him toward a new goal—perhaps one more worthy than the original goal—

by listening intently to what those little victories were telling him and where they were helping to steer his ship.

Many companies and folks chugging along in their careers miss clear opportunities because they are blinded by the main target. They fail to smell the flowers along the way—the same flowers that could have a greater bearing on their success than the original goal!

If you have come up short of your target, now is the time to start thinking creatively about the problem. If you are a company, try looking at your product or service. Maybe it's better burgers. Maybe it's a free month of service for new clients. Maybe it's a no-contract option for customers. For your career, try looking at your most recent victories and see if they are pointing you in a direction different from your main goal. What if your goal is to run the finance department and be a chief financial officer but your most recent little victories come easier to you in project management or planning? Perhaps it's time to reassess your main goals and let the little victories guide you to a new main goal.

The analytical outlook is focused on only one main target, but The Creator Mindset shakes things up and makes you focus on all the individual little victories along the way. Sometimes we don't make it to our target, and that's okay. If you feel that you don't have any little victories along the way, you are not looking hard enough. Looking—and I mean *really* looking—for the little victories allows you to define success on your own terms and in your own meaningful way. At the end of the day, a shift in your mentality away from the big win and to sustained, manageable, and repeatable little victories will allow a culture of creativity to manifest in everything that you do.

Also, it will give you options to grow as little victories become the canary in the coal mine, an early indication of where you should be paying more attention and steering your company or career.

Little victories are easy to achieve and easy to create if you start modestly. When we hold one big victory as the only possible goal, we lose the opportunity to hear what all the little victories along the way have to say, and their influence on where we end up could be profound.

dr. fleming

The Value of Making Mistakes

THE YEAR 1928 was a rough one. In the aftermath of World War I, Europe saw the rise of fascism and Nazism.[1] The world was on the brink of the Great Depression that occurred between the two world wars, and the United States was entering one of its most trying times as a nation. This was a time to get it right as mistakes would be catastrophic in one of the most perilous times in the history of the world.

Enter the most unlikely of heroes: Dr. Alexander Fleming.[2] Fleming was a scientist who was working on finding a cure for the common flu. Unsuccessful and frustrated after trying over and over to create a pill that would cure influenza, he left all of his lab equipment in place and went on vacation. There he made a life changing-mistake: He didn't clean up his gear. He just left everything as it was and took off for the vacation.

This will go down in history as one of the most important mistakes of all time.

Days later, Fleming returned to a lab with equipment showing a peculiar mold. He then had a creative idea. He thought, What if I try to do something with this mold? What if I look at it under a microscope? This wasn't standard thinking. He hadn't learned to think like this in school. It was a risk. He was being creative. He was allowing mistakes to be made without knowing what the ultimate outcome would be because mistakes can be the catalyst for something unexpected, something unknown, something profoundly important.

What he saw under his microscope forever changed the course of history. He found that inside the petri dish was a mold that ate bacteria. The particular mold he discovered was penicillin,[3] which eventually led to the discovery of antibiotics. Today he is remembered as one of the finest scientists who ever lived. He saved millions of lives all over the world because of antibiotics, but the route he found to this cure was anything but linear. It was creative, and most important, it was a mistake.

The physicist Joseph Henry once said:

> The seeds of great discoveries are constantly floating around us, but they only take root in minds well-prepared to receive them.[4]

Prepare your mind well for allowing mistakes in all you do; you might even save lives because of it. Thinking creatively often depends on making the most of your mistakes. Doing this has the potential to turn mistakes into what I call *mistake utility*: the understanding of how mistake become worthwhile.

UTILIZING YOUR MISTAKES

Mistake utility is a concept that allows you to see the value of mistakes. Those mistakes may turn out to be more than you have ever hoped for or even spark a new way of looking at things. But that is only possible if you look at mistakes as a form of wealth that is to be appreciated and valued, a utility that is to be treasured. Most people unfortunately follow the analytical view of mistakes, in which they are seen as things to be avoided at all costs.

The pessimistic and negative view that mistakes are to be shunned and never repeated for fear of getting it wrong is costly in any business or career. Actually, mistakes are really a breeding ground for innovation. This is one of the cornerstones of The Creator Mindset.

The world is filled with happy accidents and mistakes that allow for this product or that opportunity to be created from the ashes of an error. Your goal in business and in your career is to recognize mistakes as opportunities. It is critical not to go down the rabbit hole of a preordained view of the world that eliminates any creative opportunity for success.

The Creator Mindset allows for mistakes to be made because mistakes are the very foundation of creativity. When we lift away the fear of making a mistake, we give ourselves permission to explore, to push, to spread our wings and see what is out there, and to create. Analytical thinking focuses solely on a predetermined result in which only one thing should happen. Creative thinking focuses on the potential results in which many things can happen. With making mistakes comes the freedom of not having to get it right all the time, and in that freedom lies the spark of innovation.

What kind of creativity can you come up with if the fear of making a mistake is gone?

I'd like for you to think about this: What in your career or company has recently gone wrong and turned into some kind of mistake? Is it a transaction with a client in which you made some mistake on the paperwork? Is it a delivery that did not go as planned? A missed deadline? Not ordering in time for the big rush? No matter what the mistake was, it's far more important to see what you can do with that mistake now that it's over. There may be a quick rush to judgment or a search for someone to blame after a mistake is made, but what if you were to change your view on the mistake and look at it for a creative opportunity instead? What if you see its mistake utility? Go ahead and do it now. Look at the mistake that was made in a new way and see what creative spark you can derive from it.

If we take a moment to pause and look at the results with creativity in mind, we can see what the results are really telling us. Use the empathy, humor, and courage we talked about in Chapter 8 to create your own little victory and help uncover an unanticipated result in this mistake. The way we look at the results, no matter how unexpected or undesired they appear to be at first, is very powerful creatively because how we perceive the results, especially when they don't go our way, is the playground of The Creator Mindset.

Remember, The Creator Mindset allows you to see things as they can be, not as they are. Seeing potential instead of mistakes can have a lasting and profound impact not only on your business but especially on your bottom line. Think of this tool as mistake utility in which a mistake becomes a currency you can trade.

MAXIMIZE YOUR MISTAKE UTILITY

Here are three things you can do right now to maximize the value of mistake utility in your career or company:

1. Stop.

2. Learn to love imperfection.

3. Rethink the outcome.

Stop

For one minute, stop your endless charge to reach goals and aspirations. Instead, really take stock of your surroundings and ask yourself what mistakes or errors have occurred lately and what they are telling you. Start looking for the valuable clues that led to what happened. Take pause: start really paying attention. I know it's hard to look within instead of blaming someone or something else for your shortcomings, but doing this will allow you to let the error earn value by seeing it creatively.

Learn to Love Imperfection

In our race to get better and better at everything while producing faster and faster, it is essential to view things from the vantage point of potential. What I mean is that so much time is spent on tweaking an extra 0.01 percent of productivity out of an existing system or structure that we are not looking at the creative potential of what these imperfections tell us. The potential of creative genius is the imperfection of creative growth and creative power. Yet when we spend all our time looking to increase productivity in one specific realm, with blinders on, we lose sight of imperfections that can boost a new form of creativity.

Rethink the Outcome

Preconceived notions of what you think the results should be when you start a project run counter to the tenets of The Creator

Mindset. Move forward with a project but let the outcome speak for itself. You might be surprised by what it tells you (as long as you're willing to really listen).

Let go of what the outcome *should* or *could* be and instead accept that the outcome just might be a mistake. That's okay. How many times have we focused only on the result and not been creative enough to see the potential of the result? We are so keen to control our destiny that we try to control the result at all costs. It's like shooting ourselves in the foot. What we are missing is the opportunity for creativity to take hold and present a result that is something other than the preordained vision we think we need. Mistakes have the potential to lead to an even better outcome if you can learn to think about them in a creative way.

■   ■   ■

SURE, NOT ALL MISTAKES can have the same impact on the world as that of antibiotics, but mistakes of all sizes should become an important and celebrated success. Take the invention of the Post-it, for example: it too was a mistake (and one I'm personally grateful for because I can't tell you how much I love Post-its).

In 1971, engineers at 3M were trying to invent a superstrong glue. Instead, they came up with a superweak glue that became the foundation of the Post-it franchise—a franchise born out of a mistake.[5]

Safety glass was invented by mistake as well. In the early 1900s, the French chemist Edouard Bénédictus accidentally dropped a glass flask that was coated with a plastic called cellulose nitrate, and surprisingly it didn't shatter.[6] Now just about every kind of glass has this plastic on it to help prevent shattering. Think of how many lives this mistake saved by protecting occupants in cars from shattered glass.

In the late 1930s, a woman named Ruth Wakefield ran out of an ingredient while making cookies and substituted a bar of chopped-up chocolate instead. She invented the Toll House cookie (then called the Toll House Chocolate Crunch cookie) entirely by mistake.[7]

These are just a few stories of mistakes turning into utility. I could have filled many volumes with other examples. The point in all these examples is that folks who were pursuing some goal and trying to make the smallest number of mistakes possible could have given up and quit when things did not go their way. Most of them would have, including me. I know you may be thinking, Those guys got lucky. My company makes mistakes all the time, but we lose money. I get that, and the truth is that not all mistakes can be lucrative all the time. Some business mistakes can be devastating, as we will see later in Chapter 20. But rebound not only is possible, it can far outweigh the downside if you are open to looking at things with The Creator Mindset.

the ego

Art and the Ego

ART

THERE IS A stark difference between art and creativity that is not well understood. We tend to think that art and creativity are the same, but they are not, and it's important to understand why.

Art is really a small subset of creativity, and because art represents such a small fraction of the creative potential that we all have, equating art and creativity can be very dangerous to the limitless potential of creativity.

For example, if creativity were a building, art would be one piece of plywood. Sure, it's important to have that one piece of plywood in the building, but when we look at the big picture, the wood is in fact a very small component of the entire building.

Even though art is such a small subset of creativity, within art we have tons of subcategories that enhance our lives and enrich our experiences as human beings. This art affects all of our senses: sight, smell, touch, taste, and sound. We have music, sculpture, fine art, and dance, among other things, that allow for self-expression and gratification for the people who create them.

When I say art is a subset of creativity, consider that as a startling point. I mean that art has touched countless lives—I would argue that this includes just about each and every soul on Earth—yet it's only a tiny fraction of potential creativity. That is incredible, and once you see it, you can truly see how powerful and grand creativity can be.

Why do we equate art with creativity? To answer that, we need to go back to childhood.

It was easy to equate art to creativity as children because art is the very first exposure we have to creativity. Art is the first instance of creativity that is approachable and understandable to us, and there is nothing wrong with that. It is in fact a very good thing! In Chapter 3 we did an exercise in which we drew a flower because art can often be the catalyst for great creative thought. It is perfectly all right to start the journey into creativity from the base of art, but at some point art alone cannot express the limitless creative potential we all have deep inside us no matter who we are and no matter what we do.

Something interesting happens as we age: we lose the ability to differentiate between creativity and art. We think creativity is only art, and as a result, we cheat ourselves out of the wide breadth of creativity as a whole.

The consequences are dire.

We figure that art is creativity, and so we stop fostering any development of creativity. But that is a travesty. It is quite literally the belief that one piece of wood in an entire home is a good enough representation of our creative potential. That's damaging and simply not true.

The truth is that creativity is the basic building block of creating revenue and igniting a long-dormant part of the mind to reawaken the full human potential. It is innovation (a much larger subcategory of creativity than art, by the way), solutions to real problems, profit enhancement, endless growth in one's career, and so much more. In other words, creativity provides solutions that fit a real need. Creativity in my method helps people push for solutions that can be of value and service to all. The type of creativity you will find in The Creator Mindset is laser-focused on making you more money, improving your exposure, and building your brand while fusing your mind into one superunit that unleashes all human potential.

THE EGO

No conversation about art is complete without looking into the ego. The ego is defined in the dictionary as "a sense of self-worth, a sense of self-esteem, or one of self-importance." It drives artists to complete their work no matter what they are doing, from painting to music and beyond. The ego assures artists that what they are doing is a just and right expression that is worthy of completion. We can see how some dose of ego is a good thing.

But sometimes *some* ego becomes *far too much* ego, and not just for the artist. You and I and everyone we know can see that sometimes ego can get out of hand. I personally see this inflated sense of ego crippling the success of many businesses and careers today. Inflated ego can come from a person, a group, or a work culture. What we need is a recipe for how creativity views the inflated ego and what it can do to help control it, because when ego gets out of hand and goes from useful to inflated, it ends up being damaging to creativity.

What can we do about inflated egos? We need some tools from The Creator Mindset to help control it and help us catch this inflated sense of self before it can wreak havoc on our organizations and careers. This inflated sense of ego can have the tragic effect of shutting down creativity entirely, and so we must look deeper and learn three techniques to help us understand why inflated ego takes hold and what we can do about it. But first we need to look at how we can control inflated ego.

Controlling the Inflated Ego

The fact is that the complete banishment of inflated ego from an organization is a futile goal. Isn't that horrible? It will never happen, and it pains me to say that. Therefore, instead of removing ego entirely, make your goal to *reduce* it as much as possible so that creativity has a chance to flourish and take hold.

Inflated ego reduction is something we can control. We just need a little background on how it gets out of control and what we can do about it. The development of an inflated ego is directly tied to these three things I have identified below. These techniques to combat and reduce the inflated ego will work in any organization or any career no matter what your business does or where your career is headed.

1. Inflated Ego Is Tied to the Good Old Days

In many ways, inflated ego develops on top of a previous success or two. This is very important to recognize. There is no business anywhere in the world that has continued to survive unless at some point it had some success. The same thing is true of any career. It is probable that you would have been fired if you didn't have a previous success or two. That success could be big or small. It could be incremental or a tidal wave of success. But no matter how much success you've had so far, there is a foundational aspect that one thing or many things have happened at some point in the timeline of the company or career that have given you the ability to keep the lights on.

We fool our ego into believing that we have had these successes because we "know what we are doing," and that is the basis for not wanting to change anything or learn anything new; an inflated ego is the result. This becomes particularly damaging in the implementation of creativity because creativity depends on having a flexible viewpoint. Being open to different opinions and a diversity of information allows creativity to emerge. You cannot have a flexible viewpoint if your ego will not look at your mistakes creatively and use Chapter 8's unlikely personality traits of humor, empathy, and courage and the host of other tools The Creator Mindset has to allow creativity to work for you.

The belief in the good old days must be challenged and challenged repeatedly. This starts with allowing success to be appreciated but not falling in love with one's ego at every turn. It's a personal decision that we have to make. It's about viewing success in terms of little victories, not as a final milestone or arrival to serve up to our inflated egos. Only then will we find that ideas begin to be generated everywhere if we are brave enough to look. To counter the mentality that an inflated ego creates by believing that yesterday is far better than tomorrow, we must use creativity to free ourselves from the shackles of yesterday. Question past success and question future success. This keeps the ego in balance and prevents it from becoming inflated.

2. Inflated Ego Is Tied to the Structure of the Organization

Ineffective leadership in any section of a business leads to hurtful inflated ego. As an inadequate manager's ego tries to stay in control, that manager increasingly will use ego to try to maintain order. Managers like this want to keep their little turf, and any threat to that is shut down, and so they develop an inflated ego. Because any threat is shut down, creativity is unable to take hold because it's a threat to their turf. This is a vicious cycle that forever prevents creativity from starting.

If you are an employee stuck in this cycle, the only way out is creativity as a method of generating fresh and new ideas. Because creativity tends to work in tangential and nonlinear ways, you may not see immediate success. You may not see an immediate impact. But that's okay because the true power of creativity is not a cause-and-effect outcome—I do *this*, and therefore *that* happens—but a long-term haul of try and try again. It's grit. And if you are stuck under someone who is protecting his or her inflated ego's turf island, adherence to creativity to elevate the power of the idea will work eventually. It may not happen in the way that you expect, but it will happen eventually because creativity is the antidote for all darkness in ego.

If you are in a leadership position, you must recognize that these inflated ego turf islands develop as one piece of the business amasses too much authority, success, or even failure. It's amazing that failure generates inflated ego just as much as success does, but it's indeed the case. Creativity demands a constant and regular vigil over all the parts of a business, because the minute you allow a part of the business to run without challenging and adjusting it with creativity, you have set up that part to develop eventual ego cancer. What ends up happening is that any success or failure a particular part of the team has inevitably leads to a lethargic response, a silo that is deemed good enough. "It's working in some respect, so leave it alone," an inflated ego says. There is a tendency to rest upon success, a topic we will cover in far more depth in Chapter 17, but it is your responsibility in leadership to maintain an ever-growing, ever-changing, and ever-flexible path of creativity in your organization so that inflated egos do not run rampant and have a chance to develop these silos. It is also tied to comfort, which we shall see is a place where inflated ego loves to hide.

3. Inflated Ego Will Always Look for Someone Else to Blame

When one is dealing with inflated ego, the search for the culprit is always external. I have heard it all. The most common include "my clients are difficult," "the economy sucks," "it's a race to the bottom with these margins," and a personal favorite, "my boss is an idiot!" I'm sure you can come up with a few of your own reasons why you cannot achieve your goals. But the ability of creativity to ascend over an inflated ego requires that you look within.

The inflated ego has a tough time looking within and is always looking elsewhere for the problem, and so one thing you can do right now is stop blaming others for your lack of success. Take responsibility and admit that perhaps your inflated ego has gotten in the way once or twice at the very least. You cannot begin any real embrace of creative principles if you do not believe in your culpability for your own actions. If you take a minute to think of the last time you blamed someone else for your own shortcomings, you can see the inflated ego at work.

So what can you do? Contact that person and apologize and make it right in your own way. It will be painful, difficult, and uncomfortable, but even one act of admitting that you were wrong because of your inflated ego will lift the inglorious weight of ego from your shoulders and lessen your load as you progress along

The Creator Mindset way. Also, increased consciousness of this issue will go a long way. Ask yourself, Did I do this because of my ego? And is it getting inflated or is it in check?

■ ■ ■

ONE OF THE GREATEST threats to the implementation of The Creator Mindset is inflated ego. No creativity can occur in any enterprise in which ego is rampant. Inflated ego begins to erode the very foundation of the business and your career. As corrosive a power as anything, an inflated ego begins to chew away at any progress by establishing an analytical mentality that wills itself to not be changed. This mentality is inflexible no matter what is going on. Inflated ego ensures that you will be stuck. It is a prescription for disaster in any business and any career. Inflated ego leads to secrecy. It leads to silos. Communication breakdowns and a sense of complacency lead to the eventual death of the business and being stuck in countless ways over the course of your career.

The inflated ego road is one that does not need to be taken. There is hope! Using the three points described in this chapter will help shed light on certain problems in your business and career. And by shedding light, it will force the inflated ego to realize, perhaps begrudgingly, that maybe things are ripe for change. And in that change comes the true hope of true creativity.

Character Counts

beachside nir

I N GOOD TIMES, it's easy to be a hero. It doesn't take much effort to show fine character in fair weather. Things are going well, after all. Clients are responding and buying, your career is going well, promotions are beckoning, and margins are healthy.

But what happens when the ship takes on a bit of water (or a lot of water) and starts sinking?

In bad times, character is put to the test. From rich to poor, from hardship cases to those born with a silver spoon, everyone comes from somewhere, and where you come from defines who you are and what your character is. The Creator Mindset is designed in such a way that it magnifies the experiences that make you who you are. It channels who you are as an individual into creative strengths that are as strong as the DNA that makes you. It's as individual as anything in life. Because no two people are exactly the same, no two practices of The Creator Mindset will ever yield the same results.

Because it takes character to forge a path forward with dignity, honor, fairness, and respect when things don't go as planned, it's important to have the following three tools and mindsets so that you can thrive in hard times.

HOW TO THRIVE IN HARD TIMES

Be Yourself

No two people ever look at the same problem the same way creatively. In other words, who you are and creativity are one and the same. Creativity will allow you to attack issues in a way that only you can. Creativity gives you a distinct and unique voice.

For example, if you grew up in a home where money was scarce, you may or may not have developed a sensitivity to money issues. And the way you may or may not deal with those issues becomes a factor when it is looked at creatively. How? Because you are able to realize what your particular Achilles' heel is and—here's the important part—creatively *decide* whether to frame your view in the context of your particular past. The important thing to remember here is that creativity gives you a choice about how to view your individual circumstance.

With this in mind, you can either reject or embrace the cards you were dealt to fuel creativity. That's the beauty of creativity: it gives you a choice. Likewise, the choice you make opens up endless opportunities for creative thought to flourish as only you can express it.

Another example is a company in the manufacturing world that is regulated by government policy. You can choose to throw up your hands in frustration and blame all the issues you are having in your business on regulation. Plenty of companies do that. Or you could embrace creativity in coming up with a solution to the box in which you are locked up and through creativity redefine your limitations so that you can break through. It is a choice that is as intimate as any you can make in life, and its roots are deeply anchored in creativity. The beauty of creativity is that it gives you a choice about how to view your regulation problem and, best of all, *choose* how to solve it.

The solutions you create by using creativity will always be yours and yours alone no matter where you come from or what your circumstances are.

Question Norms

It turns out that we humans find normality comforting. We seek comfort and strength in patterns, and this is tied to our ancient quest for survival. It's how we are biologically wired.

That is why the necessity within The Creator Mindset to question established norms is very important. We will dive deeper into this in Chapter 20, but for now it's important to realize that anytime a norm is established, ensconced, always done this way, or routine is reason enough to question it. In this questioning of why things are the way they are you will uncover creative truths that are actionable. Just because we have always given away coupons to clients, that doesn't mean that this practice has to continue. Just because we have established a pattern of having meetings every Monday morning, that doesn't mean that this practice has to be continued.

In other words, there is nothing preventing you from looking at the world as you see fit through the lens of creativity. What you see is valuable. What you see is important. What you see deserves to be recognized. Because creativity is expressed so differently depending on who is doing it, determining what your view of your career or your company is becomes a deeply important and worthwhile exercise.

That's why it's important to question norms. Avoid the comfort mentality that is so prevalent in business today. Create your own path forward that is armed with creativity instead of accepting the established precedence of analytics.

Fight What Comes Naturally

If it were up to me, I'd be on a beach somewhere sipping a cold drink in the sunshine. Abject laziness is what comes naturally to me, but I know that laziness gets you nowhere in life. You have to fight that urge.

Perhaps laziness isn't what comes naturally to you and instead you like to control everything. No matter what you gravitate toward naturally, you must fight it because the expression of creativity will not come to anyone who is lured by what comes naturally, which to most human beings is the easy way out.

Creativity cannot thrive while we are dictated to by our natural biological instincts. What we need to do is fight this aspect of human nature so that we can climb out of the comfortable and familiar to enable ourselves to truly break free of analytical chains. Fighting human nature will allow us to embrace the potential our thinking has to be combined into one superunit and operate at the highest order of humanity. Giving in to comfort or routine will yield no worthwhile results.

Likewise, what comes naturally to us is the fringe view of always seeing what is wrong in the world. We are programmed naturally not to celebrate little victories (Chapter 10) or look at the world as it can be (Chapter 7). Instead, we see the fringe view that shows what is wrong or what is failing every time.

Fighting what comes naturally involves a heavy dose of creativity to conjure a more positive view that differs from what everyone else is seeing. Therein lies your advantage in any business or career. While everyone is seeing the bad, you are seeing the good. When it's far easier to be down about some mistake, you see an opportunity for growth and change. When it's far easier to call your boss an idiot, you instead look within to see what it is that you could be doing better.

Creativity is the greatest equalizer of resources ever because creativity does not rely on whom you know, your past, or how many resources you have. Creativity allows you to think beyond your current constraints and see nothing but potential. Within that process is a choice that you have to make at all stages of your life and career. What you choose underlines one of the most important of human endeavors: the chance to make creative character count.

CHAPTER 14

The Four Ps You Need for Growth

mechanic

I HAVE TWO FRIENDS who ran a small business. It was an independent automotive repair facility in Los Angeles. They catered to a particular brand of very high-end cars and did great work.

They were also creative.

It seemed that they were doing everything right, as if they were employing The Creator Mindset, and their business thrived for a while.

But then they got stuck.

Like the owners of most businesses, they figured out and catered to a need that was underserved in some way. But soon they wanted to grow. They wanted to diversify. They wanted to hire more staff and start another shop on the other side of town. They wanted to build upon their footprint and perhaps even franchise their model. Their hopes and aspirations were grand and unbounded. Yet they were not able to make any of that a reality.

Why?

Because they tended to use one or two elements of The Creator Mindset that they were particularly drawn to, one or two of the principles described in these pages that they were good at and that they liked. Then they took it further: they got very good at one or two elements and thought they had used the full potential of The Creator Mindset! There was no need to go any further. As humans, we love to do what we are good at. Any step outside of this comfort zone is tough. It is wrought with anxiety and fear. Thus, we tend to do what we are good at and sometimes excel at a few elements, but then we don't do much more. That's why my friends got stuck and did not continue to grow.

To be truly creative, we need to do more. It's not good enough simply to embrace one or two principles of The Creator Mindset and then stop. We need a device—four tools for creative growth—that will force us to ask ourselves some tough questions along our path to becoming fully immersed in The Creator Mindset. Those tough questions will act as checks and balances along the path to creative mastery. You can excel at any of the principles in this book individually much as my friends at the auto repair shop did. However, unless you can combine all The Creator Mindset principles into a growth path for your business or career, you are touching on only a fraction of your creative potential. It's time for the four Ps you need for growth:

1. People

2. Process

3. Product

4. Profit

I'm aware that there are a bunch of folks out there with their own Ps of business, but just to be clear, my four Ps are all about infusing each step with creativity. Each of my Ps is about learning how to use creativity in harmony with the analytics so that your potential for success becomes incrementally greater. Let's dive in.

1. PEOPLE

The first P deals with people. The reason people are first in The Creator Mindset is that people are the most valuable commodity that your business has and the people in your career network are the strongest connections you have. It is after all people who generate creativity, not machines, not efficacies, not tools. You are nothing creatively without people, and you have no identity without the people you choose to surround yourself with.

If you are a business, it all starts with hiring slow and firing fast. On the hiring side, find the best people you can and let them do what God gifted them with. Stay out of their way. For firing, get rid of the cancer ASAP. You are only as strong as your weakest link. When I am out consulting, most companies understand the firing part but think that the hiring part is all about finding someone with the exactly perfect résumé or experience who is laser-focused on the open position. This candidate has a long history of this job or that job that is within your field and has had a linear trajectory of experience. This is categorically wrong and an antiquated inheritance from the analytical approach to business. Creatively, to hire the best people you must look beyond the résumé. For example, to find people with leadership experience, my favorite technique is to hire folks from the military. It's quite likely that their experience is not in your field, but military hires tend to be amazing because of the methodical experience and discipline they have had in the service. Hire on the person, not the résumé.

In any career, the people you choose to surround yourself with will be your strongest connections at this job and the next. Simply put, people—and your investment in how you treat them— are one of the strongest determinants of how successful you will be. It doesn't matter if they are coworkers or vendors who are used to augment the staff or even customers. If you help, you will be helped. If you encourage, you will be encouraged. If you support, you will be supported. This may not happen instantly, but it will happen eventually.

My friends with the small business described in the opening of this chapter hired mostly the right people. Again—and this is important—you can hire mostly the right people but still not achieve the full potential of your Creator Mindset because getting one or two things right means that you are touching on only a fraction of your available creative potential. It turns out that there was one nepotism hire, a brother or a cousin, and that one rotten hire ended up doing not all that much. That led others to feel resentment. The staff pointed him out and said that if he didn't work hard, why should they?

Getting the people part of the four Ps right is essential. That is why it is listed first. Any shortcoming in the people part of the four Ps will have echoes for years that will stunt all kinds of company initiatives and career growth. As with a bug in the software of your business or career, you will forever be looking in every nook and cranny to find the problem when it could have been caught right at the start. Focus on the people part. Hire right and invest in your network.

2. PROCESS

The second P deals with process. Process is all about achieving little victories and capitalizing on all those little victories on your journey to the big win. It's about setting goals and taking clear and precise steps along the way to achieve those goals. It is step 2 in my cohesion plan. No matter how much creativity you embed in an organization or career, if there is no process to organize it, it will not lead to any meaningful goal or target. Instead it will lead to confusion and chaos.

If you are a company and you come up with a creative idea such as a new offering, without a process it will not be executed to its full potential if it is executed at all. It will instead lead you to fall backward to people issues. The staff will greet this new creative initiative with fear of change or a myriad of other resistances to innovation, and that will kill its potential. We learned in Chapter 2 that change is a very difficult thing to deal with at the workplace and in life. Instead, infuse process with creativity. Show the staff how this initiative can become interesting instead of threatening in a road map of little victories. Engage the operational elements and get the staff to buy into the idea. Encourage ownership of the idea across the organization so that it has a chance to materialize. Process enables communication to ring clearly across all the parts of an organization. It will allow you to begin to organize your initiative so that creativity gets to blossom into a real and actionable momentum instead of being just a creative thought someone has that quickly vanishes away.

Sometimes you do not have the authority to implement a companywide process, and that can be frustrating and lead to burnout. That's okay. Instead, focus on the things into which you can embed process. After all, there are some process items in your control no matter what it is that you do, things such as how you spend your time and what you prioritize or things such as how you execute a particular job and how and when you follow up. No matter what it is that you do, creating process will enable you to establish a rhythm in which creativity can shine.

My small business friends from earlier in this chapter had a rudimentary basic process. Again, you can have a decent process but still not achieve the full potential of your Creator Mindset because getting one or two things right is still touching on only a fraction of your available creative potential. In this case, their rudimentary process was fine while they were still small but could not keep up with the demands of growth. Intake paperwork had to be hand typed into a computer each time a customer pulled in even if it was a returning customer. Also, standard service items such as brakes and oil changes were performed differently by each mechanic, with no consistency. There was no standard process, no rhythm. Consistency is key to enabling the customer experience process to be predictable and helps build the identity of who you are and why it is you are worth doing business with.

3. PRODUCT

The third P deals with product: what it is that you really execute. Like most things in this book, it may seem obvious at first. However, it's counterintuitive because after so much time and immersion in the analytical world, we often have knee-jerk reactions to what we *think* we get paid for. We are blind to what our product or service really does in its entirety. Without looking at it with The Creator Mindset, we are seeing only half of what we do. Can you imagine driving a car while seeing only half the road or playing chess with only half the pieces? That is exactly what you are doing with your business if you don't look at the entire picture of your product or service with creativity.

For example, if you are in the manufacturing business and make parts with tolerances that are military-grade, are you a parts manufacturer? At first it may seem so, but that is the analytical view only. When this view is combined with the creative side of the brain, what you really do is provide a trusted and vetted part to someone who is in need of a highly specialized component. Sure, you make parts, but in a way you are in the trust business. Trust is your product, not manufacturing. Think back to the Trinity of Creativity to really capture your product.

If your career calls you to be a nurse, you may think that your duties are to take temperatures and make sure the charts are updated with intake paperwork and the like. It may be easy to see your role as a series of care-based executions that you perform. At first, it may seem that indeed that is what you do. But that is the analytical only view. When you look at it creatively, a whole new world begins to emerge that drives meaning into the product of your career. I would argue that most nurses are in the business of communication, being able to talk to patients so that they understand what is going on and being the glue of the patients' journey. Sure, you may take temperatures or engage in some care, but in a way you are really in the communication business. Viewed creatively, communication is your career product as a nurse, not taking temperatures or updating charts.

Defining your product, whether it's what you do as a career or what your business provides, opens up a universe of creative potential. It allows you to come up with a creative definition of what it is you do, and in that creative definition you open up a world of possibility. In a career, that may manifest as a raise or a promotion or the redefinition of your role as something exciting, new, or different. It will allow you to uncover new truths that have been unseen and make you a valuable asset to any organization. In a business, this creative product definition will enable shocking growth as you energize the direct core of the meaning of your product or service with the audience that consumes it.

To continue with the example from the opening of this chapter, the small business didn't fully understand its product. They understood some parts of it and did very well with a few parts of it but didn't understand their business as a whole, leading them to achieve only a fraction of their creative potential. They especially didn't fully understand their creative meaning. Was it fixing cars? Doing scheduled maintenance on parts subject to wear and tear? Putting extra air in the tires? Looking at it creatively, I'd say no. This business catered to people who wanted to own fancy cars at a reasonable cost. They were in the business of enabling the dream of supercar ownership without expensive maintenance for people who couldn't otherwise afford to own and maintain a fancy car. Sure, they fixed cars, but their product was enabling dream car ownership for people who otherwise could not afford it.

4. PROFIT

Finally, we have the fourth P, which deals with profit. A true derivative of getting the other three Ps right, it is the last milestone toward realizing the fruits of your labor. No matter how much creativity you embed in an organization or career, if there is no profit left over at the end of the day, you have not created a meaningful goal.

It's important to pause here and talk a little about profit and how it is analytically perceived in general. It is sometimes a difficult topic because profit is seen as greed and therefore something that is not worth our effort. But when we look at it creatively, all this talk about greed begins to unravel.

When one looks at profit creatively, an altruistic view begins to emerge. Profit allows you, whether in a business or in a career, to spend money on something you deem important. I delivered a keynote at an annual sales gathering of a company that donated 10 percent of its profits to employee-chosen charities. How awesome is that? I met a Fortune 100 company executive who gave roughly half his salary to cancer research. How amazing! Would you qualify that as being greedy or doing something that is not worth pursuing? I doubt it. Being able to do these things is a worthwhile and important matter that has its roots in profit. After all, if there is no money left over to do things with (charity, buying something, etc.), our contribution to society at large has been cut short. Far too often, profit gets bogged down with antiquated analytical views of it as a greedy or avaricious goal, but when looked at creatively, profit changes into a positive element for all.

It is time we began to get comfortable with profits and what they mean not only to our business or career but to the community at large. We can start doing this today. In a way, thinking creatively about profit allows you to work toward a goal that touches many lives in ways you cannot begin to imagine or comprehend, because everything you buy and spend money on affects other people's ability to create their own meaningful goals. This is true no matter what you spend profit on: a fancy car or a new wardrobe or a donation to charity.

For my small business friends, profit was something that was not fully realized. Although revenue was strong, waste was created at every step of the spectrum across people, process, and product. Again, you can excel at any of the principles of this book one by one, but unless you can combine them all into a path for your business or career, you are touching on only a fraction of your creative potential. Therefore, my friends realized only a fraction of their potential profit and did not realize the hard-fought equity they were lacking to expand, franchise, and realize their dream of continued and sustainable growth.

■   ■   ■

THE CREATOR MINDSET DEPENDS on viewing profit creatively and positively to allow the fruits of your labor to affect others for good. This is the fundamental shift in mentality that is required to fully grasp all the four Ps in a way that leads to growth and innovation in sustainable ways. At the end of the day, you must think that profit is a worthwhile goal and its pursuit a valuable, meaningful, and important task. At the end of the day:

> If you don't have the right *people* around you who are empowered to achieve creative greatness, the right *process* in place to allow creative ideas to become commonplace and the new normal, and if a *product* or service that is meaningfully understood by those who consume it, you will never get to a place where *profits* can benefit you and your community at large.

Following the four Ps of The Creator Mindset will open up a path for you that is repeatable and enduring. It will let you weather all kinds of storms that could derail you from innovation and sustainability. At the end of the day, my four Ps will allow you to fulfill your dreams with the power of creativity.

PART IV

SUSTAINING YOUR CREATOR MINDSET

Like anything worthwhile in life, The Creator Mindset needs to be maintained and practiced. Just as a car needs an oil change from time to time, think of the following chapters as regular scheduled maintenance of The Creator Mindset.

The Disease of Self-Doubt

dr. alexander

THERE'S A DISEASE that kills far more people than any illness. It's a disease that lives in all of us, lying dormant and waiting for the right moment to strike. It's a monster that spreads crushing self-doubt. It is the monster that attacks me while I'm writing these words. Is this chapter good enough? Is my editor going to hate it? Should I delete that last sentence? It's a natural disease that confronts everyone, but The Creator Mindset has several solutions designed to control this monster we call self-doubt.

When looked at in the context of The Creator Mindset, self-doubt is really a disease of inaction. It's a paralyzing form of introspection in which we guess and then second-guess our actions to the point of dreadful inaction. It catches us and prevents us from taking the leap into creativity. It is a disease that leads to a lack of belief in our God-given creative abilities and therefore extinguishes creativity.

Self-doubt affects each and every profession from medicine to manufacturing, from finance to technology. The analytical mindset pushes us to answer in absolute terms only. It pushes us to activate only one part of the mind in the search for an answer. It shuns any creative input that can arise from thinking in a different and unique way. As such, it continues to rob countless people, professionals, and businesses of their potential for the betterment of everyone everywhere.

Dr. Kenneth Alexander is the chief of infectious diseases at a prominent children's hospital in the United States. He has established himself as a leading authority on all kinds of pediatric infectious diseases. He studies things such as human papillomavirus and influenza. He gives talks around the world on his unique approach to infectious diseases. To say that he has a lot to lose when it comes to thinking creatively is an understatement. But one day Dr. Alexander stumbled on a creative idea so radical, so out there, that it just might change the approach to cancer treatment forever. However, self-doubt in his case created a deep worry that any new idea would put his hard-earned reputation at risk.

Dr. Alexander was studying the Zika virus, which is carried by a female mosquito. Zika is really dangerous for humans, especially babies. It causes things such as low birth weight, disfiguration, brain development issues, and possibly even death before a baby is born.

But Dr. Alexander eliminated all self-doubt and instead looked at the Zika virus as not just as a plague for developing infants but what he saw was a new cancer treatment[1] that might possibly eliminate cancer.

Despite his training and study of infectious diseases, Dr. Alexander took a leap of faith alongside his colleagues Dr. Tamarah Westmoreland and Dr. Griffith Parks. This was not a small leap in thinking; it was a massive and risky leap. But he knew that self-doubt had to be conquered, and thinking creatively has the potential to empower ideas that cannot be seen with the analytical mind alone. Against all odds and with the dedication of his team, he started to use the Zika virus to kill cancer cells in cultures in his lab. And kill cancer it did. More recently, he showed that the Zika virus can kill cancerous tumors in animal models. Once sufficient evidence is compiled, he and his team will begin initial trials to treat cancer in children. What an incredible story of creative thinking conquering self-doubt to change the world.

At any point Dr. Alexander could have given in to conventional thinking and self-doubt. Whereas most of us would have given up because we don't want to risk our reputation or succumb to doubt, he worked creatively to create a breakthrough of epic proportions.

Why is this so important to understand? Because where comfort is pervasive, self-doubt thrives.

Modernity has brought on a host of comfortable conveniences that are life-changing. In the past several hundred years the human quest for survival has moved away from being a day-to-day struggle and into the relatively comfortable existence we know today. Where there is comfort, there is an abundance of time to question our actions. And when we question our actions over and over, inaction then drives us away from creativity and into doubt.

Today around the globe there is no longer a need just to survive. In that abundance of time spent away from dealing with sustenance each and every waking moment, there is plenty of time for self-reflection, self-analysis, and self-introspection, all of which could lead to crippling self-doubt and inaction in terms of creativity.

Harriette, our cavewoman from Chapter 6, didn't have time for self-doubt. Every waking moment was a fight for survival. She moved from kill to kill, from shelter to shelter, from water source to water source. Her only goal in life was to survive and ideally have children. But today comfort is prevalent in almost every corner of the globe. With all this time on our hands, away from the immediate needs of survival, we are prone to overthink, overprocess, and overanalyze. Self-doubt lies waiting for us to have enough time to think about what we are doing and question it. Over and over, like a vicious cycle of self-attack, we are drawn in with no end in sight. Small doubts begin to become bigger. Cracks become valleys. Self-loathing becomes the norm. Pretty soon the fear paralyzes us, and so we do nothing risky, nothing new, nothing creative.

As you might have guessed by now, self-doubt tends to live in the analytical. Forever seeing the world as black and white, the analytical mind hesitates to offer a creative gray. All it sees is absolute. With that comes the crushing pressure to get it right, to not make mistakes, to hit the bull's-eye time and time again, to execute flawlessly. Because that view encompasses so little of our creative potential, it is beyond question that we carry around with us the crushing weight of self-doubt by trying to get it right all the time. Without the creative part of our human condition, we are destined to fail.

For example, you can see it play out in schools at all levels every day across the country. Teachers lecture and then ask students questions in hopes that they will receive the right answers, and this system for learning hasn't changed in a hundred years.[2] You see, most teachers are looking for the *right* answer.

Not a guess, not a conversation, not the activation of the creative mind, but another example of privileging the analytical part of the brain. This training makes us afraid of being wrong. Our testing methods are the same. We have countless assessment tests that can verify if learning is taking place, but what exactly are we verifying? These assessments are really about how students perform on taking the tests and little else.

Our schooling has conditioned us to think that if we don't know the exact answer to a question, we shouldn't participate. We shouldn't guess, we shouldn't make a sound. It does this at the worst possible time in development: during childhood, when the creative mind is supposed to run free and take shape.

Because of all this, we've created a gap between where we could be as a society and where we currently are. Of course, I'm not naïve enough to think that this is the only reason we haven't achieved more as a whole. There are certainly plenty of other issues that block our way to progress. But the overwhelming power of the disease of self-doubt is such a strong force that everyone is affected by its crippling power at one time or another, probably from a very early age.

THE THREE TOOLS TO TACKLE SELF-DOUBT

In light of the fact that we all can see how self-doubt is an ever-powerful force, I have three specific tools that you can use right now to tackle this common issue. Let's dive into each one.

1. The Faucet Tap

The faucet tap is a visualization method that not only can help you understand how ideas interact but also help you reduce the stress of having to "get it right" as we've been trained to do for so long. Here's what I'd like you to do. Imagine an open water tap that begins to flow. Each bit of water that comes out is made of millions of molecules that rush together to form water. The water does not care which molecule comes first or which molecule comes later. It doesn't stop to think about what it is; it just is.

When faced with crippling self-doubt, I often think about how water can represent a flow of ideas that is uninhibited regardless of what idea comes before it or what idea comes after it. In that moment the idea just exists.

Just as the water molecules interact without thinking about *how* to interact, your ideas can flow without there being any pressure for them to make sense immediately. When you take that pressure away, it makes it easier for you to play, to explore, to forgive, to create, and to make mistakes. Why? Because allowing your innate creativity, which has been a part of you since birth, to flow the way it did when you were a child will help loosen the grip of self-doubt.

2. The Light of Positivity

When you choose to see the positive instead of the negative, the way you look at the world will change completely. As we learned in Chapter 7, positivity will allow us to carry an idea to its full and rightful destiny, providing the fertile ground in which creativity can grow. It turns out that this fertile ground of positivity also will help banish self-doubt.

I know that you may be thinking that that's a bit nuts. I mean, who would look at self-doubt—those deeply embedded weaknesses we are all afraid of exposing—with positivity? There is nothing positive about these things! But this is important, and it works. I challenge you to stop looking at self-doubt negatively and instead shift your attitude to one that's positive. Instead of attacking yourself and stopping the flow of ideas because something is "stupid" or "will never work" or "will be viewed by my peers as fringe and too out there," allow yourself to develop options to let your ideas run free. Say to yourself that "this is just one idea of many" and remind yourself that with these newfound options you will see a subtle yet significant shift in your attitude. By allowing yourself to have options, you will slowly begin to shape your self-doubt into something more manageable.

This positivity will allow you to gather a collection of potential ideas that you don't have to act on if you don't want to. What freedom from self-doubt that brings! You can even cultivate ideas and keep them for later if you want to test-drive them at some point. Perhaps most important, positivity will allow you to burn away your self-doubt in a safe environment away from any judgment from yourself or others. What ends up happening is that you get to burn away the anxiety that comes with self-doubt in a way that gets it out of your system, and when you get it out of your system, creativity is able to take hold. When you're not reliant on just a single precious idea, you give yourself a break and allow more creative opportunities to present themselves.

3. The Shotgun

The third technique I have for dealing with the crushing weight of self-doubt is the shotgun method. This is a tool that helps you find your target and takes the edge off any attempt at perfection as a result. This technique is all about developing a bunch of ideas and seeing what sticks while banishing self-doubt.

Remember my love of Post-it Notes? It's time to get some out. Take a bunch of Post-its or any blank pieces of paper that you can tear up into smaller pieces. Once you have your supplies ready, write down each self-doubt on its own piece of paper. You can write down "I lack resources" or "I should be better or faster or more agile" or "I wish I wouldn't rush a deal or con-tract or job search" and on and on. Write these self-doubts down and get them out of your system.

You don't have to worry about getting this exer-cise right. There is no right. The doubts that you write down are yours and yours alone. Write down any doubts you may be having about anything. It may be that the first few are things that you are afraid of. It may be that the doubts you write down involve your lack of skills or lack of acquisition of a particular skill. It can be anything. This is the beginning of the self-doubt purge.

If you stick to it, soon something amazing will happen.

When you write down the elements that are giving you this doubt, pretty soon you will run out of things to write. The doubts will begin to run out, and what you will see is simply amazing: you will begin to come up with not doubts but ideas.

It may take a while or it may be quick, but that doesn't mat-ter because soon these doubts will exit your system and ideas will replace them. Once you are done, walk away from these notes for at least a day.

After those 24 hours have passed and when the time feels right, go ahead and reread what you're written. Look at your doubts and the ideas they have created. Much as a shotgun blast affects a general target, not a focused one, this method will allow you to lessen the strain of getting it right the first time and allow you to sift through a bunch of ideas that you probably would have blocked because of self-doubt. By giving yourself permission, patience, and the opportunity to explore, you will have allowed creativity to give you the power of the idea.

■　　■　　■

WE ALL KNOW THAT the burden of self-doubt can be crushing, but we also need to learn that defeating it is possible. Although almost everyone out there is thinking with the analytical side only, the future of business will be inherited by those who are able to fuse their minds into thinking holistically. This idea economy will eventually replace the antiquated industrial economy to become the new marketplace of the twenty-first century. That exciting new frontier is open to anyone who chooses to approach it creatively. Overcoming self-doubt won't just improve your business or career; it will make you and the community around you better. Follow the three steps to crush self-doubt daily and allow creativity to take hold in its place.

Comfort, Computers, and the Multitasking Myth

switching gears

WE ALL CARRY with us a mistaken belief that comfort is a good thing. We strive to live in comfortable homes. Our food is produced comfortably for us by someone else. We work to be surrounded by comfortable things. Comparing today's comfort levels with those of 100 years ago, we live pretty good lives.

However, The Creator Mindset cannot be achieved when comfort is involved or accepted. Comfort in and of itself is not the breeding ground for ideas and innovation. It's the breeding ground for complacency, which we will look at in greater detail in Chapter 19. But for now, Comfort is a deeply ingrained method of survival that acts as self-preservation. It's simply not in human nature to stick our necks out, to take risks, and to drive ourselves further. We all seek comfort and predictability in every moment of our lives. We build up anxiety when things don't go our way.

Our love affair with technology feeds into this myth, too. It operates under the false promise that it will give us what we crave the most: comfort and predictability. Many technology companies actively work on this human vulnerability. They activate dopamine sensors within all of us to "reward" us with a like here or a new app there. They prey on our genetic makeup.[1] It's no wonder we have such intense relationships with our devices.

Despite this relationship with our devices and the attempt to make us feel more connected, this increasingly makes us more and more alone. Our technology presence becomes an idealized version of ourselves that we can never hope to obtain in real life. It leads us down a rabbit hole of seeking more and more comfort that breeds more and more isolation and a greater reliance on technology. But in a world of isolation, creativity becomes more important and powerful than ever because it is the one thing that connects us to our ancestral selves. Today that is something we crave more than ever because it is real. And what is real allows us to develop a Creator Mindset. How do we get off our overreliance on technology as a false prophet and relearn creativity? I have a few tools that can help.

RELEASING YOURSELF FROM TECHNOLOGY'S GRIP

Part of The Creator Mindset includes fighting comfort and the death grip technology has on our lives. Here are six ways you can release yourself from technology's grip.

1. Schedule a Tech Detox Day

Once a week (more often would be even better), shut off all technology and detox from it. You will find amazing renewal when you step away from technology and will see how much time and energy our screens devour in the false name of productivity.

You may be tempted to think that this is a cliché or something people talk about but do not do. But this is important, and the results you see will be substantial.

Allow yourself some time to adjust to being in the moment without a phone, a tablet, the Internet, or television in your life. Then gradually increase these times away from technology so that your reliance on tech becomes more and more sporadic. You will discover that there is grace and strength in time away from your devices, and you just might find that you have more time to pay attention to the things that really matter. If you cannot shut your devices off, at least turn off the notifications from time to time. That way, you are not disturbed when you are working on getting creativity to flow.

2. Do It in Person

It never ceases to amaze me how many people try to use technology as a substitute for human interaction. There is no app or technology that can substitute for face-to-face time. Whether it's with clients, customers, or friends, being present and in person is always the best way to communicate. You may be thinking that no one has time for in-person meetings anymore and that my advice is a bit old school. But sometimes when you are thinking creatively, old-school ideas become completely new, and this is one of those times.

Travel to meet a client in person. Share a meal or a cup of coffee with a friend and spend some time together. Building relationships that do not involve technology and convenience is essential in mastering The Creator Mindset.

One of my favorite Fortune 500 companies spends an exorbitant amount on travel. They seek to do as much business as possible in person by sending folks all over the world to engage in personal meetings and conversations. You may think that it's an unsound strategy that involves spending millions a year on travel that could be replaced by technology, yet they are one of the most profitable companies in the world.

3. Accept that Multitasking is BS

Let's do a little exercise that will help us understand how to recover what we've lost as a result of technology so that we can find a better way forward with creativity.

Find a piece of paper and draw two lines a few inches apart parallel to each other. Make those lines about the length of the entire page. Take out a timer and time yourself as you write out the following sentence: "The quick brown fox jumps over the lazy dog." Don't just rush through it by writing sloppy letters; it must be legible. When you're done, write down the time it took you to write the sentence and circle it. This sentence happens to have all the letters in the alphabet.

On the line below this, write out a series of numbers. But first you will start that timer again. This time, you'll be writing every even number starting with 2 and going all the way up to 70 (2, 4, 6, 8, 10, 12, 14, 16, 18, 20, 22, 24, 26, 28, 30, etc.). Again, you must take your time and write legibly. When you're done, write down the time this took and circle it as you did with the previous sentence.

Now for the tricky part. First, I want you to flip the paper over so that you have a clean page to write on. Draw two lines on the page parallel to each other and get that timer ready to go again. This time you'll be working on both sections simultaneously. On the top line, you'll write the first letter ("T") and then write the first number ("2") in the bottom part of the page. After that, go back to the top section and write "H" and then move back down to the bottom for the "4." Keep doing this until you have competed the entire sentence "The quick brown fox jumps over the lazy dog" and the number sequence as you did before, continuing to alternate with each. Remember to keep it legible. Do this exercise as fast as you can and once again write down the time it takes to get it done and circle the final time on your page.

Once you are done, flip the page and look at both circled times you wrote down for the first parts of the exercise. Not too bad, right? Now flip back to the side of the page where you switched between numbers and letters and compare that time. That number isn't as impressive, right?

Why? Because we are terrible at multitasking.

Conventional logic (the analytical) says that multitasking should be faster, that you should be able to do two things in the same amount of time it takes to do one. But as you can see when you compare the times from doing each task individually versus doing them both at the same time, *multitasking takes far longer.*

For the record, I've tried this exercise all over the world in different cultures, with different people, different genders, and different countries, but the results are always the same.

Multitasking often takes four to eight times longer than just doing the letters and the numbers by themselves.

It turns out that doing one thing at a time and sticking to it actually is faster. The brain cannot execute both tasks with efficiency. It's actually the opposite: it's less efficient. This is a simple exercise, but it shows that multitasking is a myth.

Despite the evidence, we live in a world that idolizes multitasking. Yet as you can see with this simple exercise, multitasking is indeed a myth. Now change those tasks to real-world work tasks and you'll start to see how much productivity we've lost by thinking that we're able to multitask.

I know you're tempted to find some technology solution to help you process all the information that you deal with throughout the day. You want an app or some other technology to help you with the deadlines, the meetings, and the temptation to multitask. But there is no technology solution better than paying attention to one thing at a time! The Creator Mindset is all about focusing on one thing at a time. If you are able to do that instead of trying to multitask, creativity will fill your decision making.

4. Switch Gears

To move away from the temptation of multitasking, I challenge you to use a method I call switching gears. This method will help you deal with the ever-increasing weight that technology and multitasking put on us today. Switching gears is a tool in which you focus on one thing at a time instead of multitasking, giving one thing at a time your full and undivided attention. That's it. Then, when you are finished—and only when you are finished— *switch gears* to something else and give that your full and undivided attention

No matter how much time you spend on each gear or how important that gear is, give it your undivided attention. One gear might be about finance in a meeting. The next gear might be a phone call about distribution. Another gear after the finance and distribution meeting might be a discussion of hiring or human resources or a deadline coming up. All of these gear changes are essential, and creativity is the oil that lubricates the machine. How? Creativity results from focusing on one thing at a time. Changing gears allows you to concentrate on the item in front of you exclusively. Without trying to multitask, you will allow the creative mind to balance the analytical and therefore allow creative solutions to emerge.

5. Do Something Uncomfortable Today

Allow yourself to enter a situation in which you force yourself outside of your comfort zone. Do this today. Whether it is at a work meeting or a social event, step out of your comfort zone once in a while and take a risk. Force yourself to stick your neck out for something new and different.

You will notice that doing this will result in an unexpected and creative view that pushes you out of the familiar and into the unknown. In this view, you will find a new and different creative way of seeing things.

Why? You are literally forcing yourself to step outside of what is comfortable and predicable for you. It's different for everyone, and what works for you may not work for someone else.

We all have a mental inventory of things we would love to do and things we would love to try, but we probably don't do them because we prioritize comfort and push those situations off to tomorrow or next week or next year. Stop that now and start to do these things today. The mental inventory we carry around with us is chock-full of ideas we want to try or things we want to do. That is our primordial creativity trying to get out into the world. Get out there and listen to it, and do it now. Not tomorrow, not next week or next year—today.

6. Realize Tech Is Fleeting; Creativity Lasts Forever

I studied music as an undergraduate, and to this day I remember a very important lesson I learned about harmonic theory in a piano class. The theory states that each note played on a piano (or any other instrument) lasts forever—music actually lasts forever. Isn't that awesome? It means that any music ever played is still playing. Literally. It's just that the volume it plays at is ever decreasing. Yet that doesn't mean it's not there. Sure, the volume is so low that no one can hear it anymore, but think of how special it is. It means that Mozart's and Bach's music is still in the atmosphere, sounding at ever-decreasing volumes. Forever. Jimmy Hendrix's guitar is still ringing somewhere in the ether. Isn't that something? Before I lose you, let me tie this back to our discussion.

The work you generate by using your creative tools is just like harmonic theory: because it involves creativity, it will last forever.

The lives you touch from the product or service you create by using creative principles will live on forever. Don't rely on machines that are analytical code instructions that force us into predictable boring patterns. Rely on yourself and creativity for so much more.

We can give our careers and companies meaning by understanding that the creative principles we are beginning to practice live on forever. How powerful is the line supervisor at a shop that makes door thresholds when she knows that one of her products will deeply touch a buyer in a way she can't possibly imagine? She will never get a thank-you card in the mail or an online review of how this product was special. But it will happen. How powerful is your career as a delivery person knowing that one of your deliveries will change a person's life forever? And how powerful is a company that makes patio umbrellas for restaurants knowing that at some restaurant at some point in time under the shade of your product will be an epic family reunion 30 years in the making?

We seldom will ever know these things. And the fact that we cannot "hear" it—as in the harmonic theory—doesn't mean it doesn't exist. Creativity forces us to realize that there is not a direct connection between our actions and the results. We have to believe and trust *creatively* that they are occurring.

■   ■   ■

WE MAY NEVER KNOW how we affect people by the outcome of doing our jobs or running our companies. But creatively thinking about our jobs and companies just might create amazing connections. Analytically, a person is just another number on the spreadsheet, drowning in the despondency of mediocrity. But creatively, we see that everyone—no matter who—matters.

digital camera

How to Champion the Good Idea

N 1973 A man by the name of Steve Sasson went to work for Kodak. Palpable interest in all things digital was beginning to grow everywhere, and most companies wanted to know how they could get in on it.

In 1975, Steve's boss assigned him to an engineering unit to work on coming up with ideas around a recently discovered CCD (charged couple device) microchip. After exploring a few ideas that went nowhere, he got creative. He thought, What if I use these chips to capture light in some way and make a digital impression?[1] It was a new way to think and was creatively ambitious. No one had ever done that with this particular chip, and he thought to himself, What do I have to lose?

What Sasson made while thinking creatively changed the course of history forever. He wound up creating the world's first digital camera. This eight-pound device had 16 batteries, a tape cassette recorder, and several dozen circuits wired together.[2] It looked like a bomb straight out of an old cartoon, but this idea changed technology forever. It took 0.01-megapixel photos in black and white and recorded them to a tape. Each photo took almost half a minute to produce, and if you wanted to view a photo, you had to play back the tape and plug it into a television screen, which took another minute or so. The picture quality was horrible; the image was grainy and noisy and didn't look very good,[3] but none of that mattered. It was the first handheld digital camera ever invented, and it couldn't have come at a better time or in a more relevant company.

Eventually, Sasson made his way onto the leadership team at Kodak, but instead of his creativity being championed, his digital camera was not well received. No one liked or understood his invention, which was even seen as threatening. In the end, the leadership team at Kodak convinced themselves that no one would ever want to take a picture digitally and that things would stay the same forever.

Kodak filed for bankruptcy in 2012.

Kodak's story is a tragic one, but the important thing to ask here is why it happened. It turns out that a combination of things had gone wrong for Kodak that we can learn from so that they don't happen to us. When creativity occurs in our business or career, we need to be ready to capture it in all we do. What can you do to champion creativity in your career or your company? Here are a few tools that can help.

HOW TO BE A STALWART SUPPORTER OF CREATIVITY

The rest of this chapter lists techniques that will allow you to support creativity.

1. Think Like a Child

When you were a kid, you were free to make plenty of mistakes. The stakes were just not that high. If you failed in playing or dancing or just about anything else, you didn't blame yourself or the market conditions. Of course not. You just went out and tried again. Here is the important thing: when we think like a child, we are not afraid to retry what has failed.

What you end up gaining is a childlike indifference to aversion, a form of creative grit. Now it is time to use the grit you had as a kid. It's the same grit you can use as an adult to bounce back. When you think like a child, you give yourself permission to explore: to go big, to dream, and to imagine the bigger picture creatively.

Think more like a child when you are solving problems in your career or business. You will get an opportunity to push the boundaries on potential solutions and rely on your grit in dealing with failure. In those potential solutions there are opportunities to champion creativity.

One of the side benefits of thinking like a kid is the camaraderie it creates. When you give life to an idea while thinking like a child, you may ignite a following in others. Sort of like a contagious connection fueled by bucking the status quo, thinking like a child can rally support. Coworkers and customers see the need for ideas like yours that are disruptive because they were children at one point too—everyone was! There is a certain memory that is triggered by thinking like a child that is communal. Therefore, connecting to the primordial creative brain we are all born with has the ability to champion any creative idea in any organization.

2. Try Saying Yes Sometimes

I wonder what would happen at your company if an employee or coworker presented an idea like the digital camera at Kodak. How would you react? Do you think you would be able to spot the potential of this innovation? Would you be prepared to take a leap with The Creator Mindset and see the potential for something that is so fundamentally disruptive to your organization?

Sadly, the answer is probably not. We have spent so much time specializing in understanding our role in our career or our company's function that we cannot see outside the day-to-day grind. It really is true that sometimes the best ideas come from unexpected places, but are we willing to look in unexpected places for newfound creativity? Taking a leap of faith by saying yes from time to time is one way to look in those unexpected places for ideas. It is one way to see outside the daily grind.

So much time is spent saying no in business today. Try saying yes from time to time. Yes requires that you take a risk; no is always a safe way out.

No matter who you are, from the owner of the company all the way to an intern, it is your job to help champion the idea regardless of its origin.

Saying yes allows you to understand that in a world of constant change, sometimes we don't have all the answers. No is a far easier position and involves less risk. Saying yes takes far more effort, but the payoff to yes is far greater. Higher risk, higher reward, higher championing of creativity.

3. Recognize Fear

Fear of failure is a major force in driving bad business and career decisions today. As we have seen, it is in failure that creativity can shine. So why are we so afraid of it? Sometimes it is more about getting it wrong and learning than getting it right and not learning. Sure, your mistakes can lead to big issues from time to time, but I would argue that trying to get it right all the time (which is impossible) is far more costly in the long run. Creative ideas get stifled when you are on a mission to get it right all the time, and fear of the unknown leads to a paralysis of action on any risk that destroys creativity.

What fear exists in your organization or career that is preventing you from being a champion of innovation? Most folks would say that it's bad cash flow, lack of profit, or constantly decreasing margins. Maybe it's a bad boss or a lack of clear career objectives. These certainly are real fears, but they are fears that can be transcended at all levels with creativity.

Let's look at these fears quickly one by one:

1. A lack of cash flow can be changed easily if you have the right mindset. It turns out that limitations (on available cash flow in this case) force you to use creativity (which is essentially free) to transcend your current limitation and come up with a solution. You most likely don't need a loan or have to renegotiate terms on your accounts receivable; you need to look at every nook and cranny of where the cash is being spent and then implement creativity.

2. Lack of profit is a wonderful problem to have. It means you have some level of existing revenue and have not

been able to leverage it to profitability at sufficient levels. Here you look at the problem creatively to employ a solution: Is it inventory, pricing, education, or something internal that is creating this lack of profit? There are so many places to look that you are bound to strike the mother lode if you are guided by creativity.

3. Decreasing margins are another one of my favorite issues to tackle when I am out consulting. Decreasing margins are led by market forces that do not differentiate your product or service from others. Why not try creativity to overcome these limitations and differentiate with a concrete and resolute mandate? Redefine or create an evolved position and execute it.

4. If you have a bad boss, this is a great opportunity to learn. I have had some of the worst bosses in the universe (see the section on my boss Allen in Chapter 9), and I bet you have too, but here is the thing: What did you really take away? Was it resentment and bitterness? Or was it creativity to look at this person's actions and learn what not to do? As we talked about earlier in this chapter, sometimes it is more about getting it wrong and learning than about getting it right and not learning. I learned so much from Allen (the worst boss I ever had) because I chose to look at the situation creatively and not get bogged down in the mire.

5. A lack of clear career objectives provides another great opportunity to use creativity to overcome a hurdle. Define your career objectives in a way you feel is most appropriate by using creativity at every step. Embrace the idea that a laundry list of expected job performance

indicators is bestowed upon you as your job description, but then make the creative choice to do more. Look at the potential you have to push the boundaries creatively and you will find that your role can take on a whole new meaning.

The power of an idea to forever change the outlook of the market you are in is far more powerful than the limitations that you have in front of you. Ideas will always win, no matter what. Creativity will always win, no matter what. But have you given creativity the chance to bloom without fear in every facet of your career or business that drives you away from being a champion of creativity?

Finally, what are you ignoring because of fear in your business today just as Kodak did? Personally? From within? What idea did you have just last week, the one you thought was so out there that you didn't bother to share it with anyone? What creativity lies just beneath your surface that you are afraid of?

Perhaps the problem is not wanting to get it wrong. Perhaps it's not wanting to change the current trend of what is working. Perhaps the self-doubt monster is shutting it down. What is it that you can champion with creativity that you are too afraid to try? No one knows but you. If you keep it under lock and key, forever afraid of revealing your ideas, nothing will ever happen. You can take that creativity to the grave, and the impact that it would potentially have not just on your career or business but on the world will be forever unrealized.

4. Get Unstuck from a Band of Time

Nothing lasts forever, and the fact is that things work only for a certain amount of time. Whatever is working today may not work tomorrow, and whatever is working tomorrow is not necessarily a solution for the future. It is only a solution for right now based on what's familiar and what's established.

The good news is that there are two simple questions that can help you get unstuck from a certain band of time and drive yourself headlong into championing creativity. Look at what is working today and ask yourself these two very important questions:

1. Will what I'm doing *today* be relevant *tomorrow*?

2. When what I'm doing is not relevant, what can I do to *change* it?

These two very simple questions can have deep implications for your career or business in terms of championing creativity. The first one involves a real gut check of whether your product or service will be relevant in however you define your particular tomorrow (in one day from now or in one year's time or more). It's the self-check that will help you clarify an honest interpretation of your offering. Remember it's not *if* but *when* relevancy becomes questionable. Much like death and taxes, it's inevitable. So why not champion that creative initiative?

The second question deals with the inevitable: when relevancy is no longer a factor. It asks what you can do to *change* so that you can stay relevant. It questions how much creativity you can champion so that the change becomes a force in your company or career. The answer will be individual to you and your career or business sector and will be found in whatever creativity you can champion by using the principles described on these pages.

Forever pushed out of a position of comfort, The Creator Mindset encourages looking at your business with new and inventive eyes and driving hard to champion a good idea no matter where it comes from. This in no way means that you should ignore your current model. But if all you are doing is working on your current model, you are not in a position to capitalize on change.

As things occur only in some optimal band of time or some limited amount of time, creativity will help you reinvent yourself in your career or your company's product or service to continually be fresh, new, and relevant. Go out and find or make it and then champion it to success.

5. Do Not RUST

The rest upon success tool (RUST) is one of the only tools that I will cover in this book that I do *not* want you to use. You cannot possibly act as a champion of creativity if you rest upon success.

The Creator Mindset is built to fight our natural urge to rest and say, "Why fix what isn't broken?" This destructive force is no longer constructive in any meaningful way, and this tool is one that has to be unlearned. Resting upon success is exactly what Kodak did, along with Toys "R" Us, Pan Am Airlines, and Columbia House, as you will learn in Chapter 19. It's the anti-advocate of creativity. This is a culture that reveres past success and doesn't see anything worthwhile in the future to pursue, not to mention that it makes employees feel that ideas will never be taken seriously, investors feel leery and disengaged, and the public feel lethargic and indolent. In the culture of a company steeped in the past, creativity that bubbles up is shut down. These types of environments that lack a champion of the idea to stand up collectively and defend creativity eventually are out of business. Creativity is the very fabric of our humanity, and ignoring it because it might not happen in the next 5 or 10 years or because you just don't get it is no reason to stop progress. You are simply robbing the next generation of innovation and creativity at your own expense and leading to the eventual downfall of your organization.

■   ■   ■

THE CREATOR MINDSET IS set up to allow the championing of creativity whether it appears as an idea, an innovation, a new way of thinking about something, or the countless other ways creativity can manifest. No matter where it comes from, creativity must be supported. It is not good enough to create an environment where these ideas can be generated. They must be upheld in every way.

tylenol

The Creator Mindset
Guide to Crisis

T WAS A school day seemingly like any other on September 29, 1982. Twelve-year-old Mary Kellerman from Elk Grove Village just outside of Chicago woke up with a bad sore throat and a runny nose. She was a typical kid, and her symptoms were not remarkable in any way. She didn't feel well enough to go to school that day, and her parents agreed to keep her home. They gave her some Tylenol and encouraged her to go back to bed, but they soon found her lifeless on the bathroom floor.[1]

Adam Janus woke up that same fateful morning of September 29, 1982, also not feeling right. A father of two young children and the son of Polish immigrants looking for a better life in the United States, he had worked hard to get a mail route for the U.S. Postal Service and was proud of his position.[2] He had some muscle pains after a particularly grueling route the day before.

He went to the drugstore first thing in the morning and bought a bottle of Tylenol. He took two pills and headed home, and within hours he was found dead on his bedroom floor.

Mary Reiner wanted to be a mother her whole life. She had just returned home from the hospital after giving birth to a baby, but that joyous occasion was marred forever by tragedy. She took Tylenol to help ease some of the pains of her recent childbirth. Hours later, she was found in a coma and rushed back to the same hospital where she had given birth; she was pronounced dead shortly after arriving.[3]

■   ■   ■

THINGS WERE GOING VERY well for Johnson & Johnson in early 1982. Their stock was rising to new highs,[4] internal investments were beginning to realize profits after long and expensive runs in development, and their pain reliever Tylenol was reaching epic market shares. In fact, 17 percent of Johnson & Johnson's entire revenue was generated from Tylenol and related products.[5] It was and still is the most frequently prescribed pain reliever in the world, and it seemed that the sky was the limit for the company at that time.

But sometimes crisis happens, and it often happens at the worst possible time. The thing that helps most in any crisis is trust.

I can see how it might have been easy at Johnson & Johnson to get smug with all that success; it was, after all, one of the most prosperous times in company history and creativity was flowing. But any sustainable practice of The Creator Mindset relies on humility to make it all work when things don't go as planned. Humility builds trust. And for trust to be implemented successfully, it needs to become a creative tool.

Trust and humility are indeed tools your career or company can implement with creativity, and later in this chapter we will see how. We often think of innovation or ingenuity as being a product or service enhancement, but innovation also can be the creation of trust. What Johnson & Johnson wound up doing in 1982 in the midst of that crisis has forever changed the paradigm of trust and what it means for a brand to be trustworthy.

James E. Burke was Johnson & Johnson's CEO at that time. He was named by *Fortune* magazine as one of history's 10 best CEOs. However, it wasn't for his track record with the board of directors or some new hiring method and it wasn't for his fortuitous investments. It was for his handling of a terrorist attack. A terrorist forever disrupted the landscape of trust in America when he or she tainted a number of Tylenol products with cyanide. And James Burke's strong and decisive leadership at one of Johnson & Johnson's worst times will forever make him a master of The Creator Mindset.

If you are ever in a situation in which you need to rebuild after a crisis, these are the steps that James took and that you should too.

1. BE VULNERABLE

James Burke immediately showed that Johnson & Johnson was vulnerable when he explained at a press conference that the company didn't know what exactly was going on but that they were all working feverishly to uncover the culprit.

It turns out that a terrorist had tainted Tylenol bottles with cyanide for no reason other than to scare the public. The terrorist murdered Mary Kellerman, Adam Janus, and Mary Reiner, and would go on to murder five more people.

As soon as Johnson & Johnson knew that the pills had been tainted, they communicated it to the mass media even though the pills had been tampered with after they left the factory. Technically, Johnson & Johnson was not to blame, but that didn't matter because the damage had already been done. Sharing what Johnson & Johnson knew was a risky decision because they didn't know much, but they knew that they had to update the public to rebuild trust. Even as investigators were doing their work, the company updated the public with information as it was uncovered. They didn't wait for the whole story to be in; they were vulnerable and open at all times during the crisis.

Why does being vulnerable work creatively? Because in any career or business, when we allow ourselves to shed the steel coat of impenetrability and let ourselves be vulnerable, we tap into the primordial mind that connects people at the deepest level. Why? Because being vulnerable is universal. It is something that we all feel at some point in our lives, and it resonates as a human truth. This is an incredibly powerful position to be in. Imagine something happening in your business or career that is completely out of your control. Now imagine taking a position of vulnerability to ensure the public that you are doing your very best and are working toward a resolution.

Today we are too worried about how we may look or how we may be perceived if we are vulnerable because we often equate vulnerability to weakness. But what we are missing is the hidden creative power that allows you to relate on a human level because no one is perfect and everyone knows that. In other words, the customer, client, buyer, and boss know you aren't perfect because they aren't perfect either. That very vulnerability sets you up for the creative tool that is *relatability*.

There was a transparency at Johnson & Johnson that resonated with consumers. They felt they were uncovering the act of terror *together*. James Burke's decision to address the world long before all the facts were released gave the general public the feeling that everyone was on the same team. That created a sense that everyone was responsible for helping to bring this act of terror to an end. Johnson & Johnson was demonstrating that they didn't have all the answers and that sometimes vulnerability in the wake of a crisis is the most honest and refreshing approach. Even such a large corporation as Johnson & Johnson was susceptible to shortcomings in a time when information was scarce, and this resonated with the public.

The next time something like this happens in your business or career—and heaven forbid that it be this bad—use creativity to show that you are vulnerable. By using directness and candor in your approach, you will find that most people understand that the human condition is far from perfect and that we're all in this together.

2. RESTORE TRUST AT ALL COSTS

James Burke instructed the plant that made Tylenol to shut down the production line for the capsules. They even cleared store shelves of the product amid ghastly evening news stories and photos. Even though Johnson & Johnson was 100 percent sure that the pills had not been tampered with at the factory, they mandated that no more manufacturing or sales would be done until they could get to the bottom of what was going on. At the costs of millions of dollars, it was effectively the first recall in history. But James Burke and the leadership at the company steadfastly maintained that earning trust was far more important than revenue.

TV pundits at the time had written off Tylenol as a brand forever. They said that no one would ever buy one pill of Tylenol ever again[6] and that Johnson & Johnson was doomed as a result of this act of terror. But internal leadership didn't listen and continued to hold true to its goal of restoring trust at any cost.

Restoring trust at all costs is a very important tool we can learn from in our businesses or careers. It turns out that if you are looking at things creatively when times get tough and there is a crisis, there is a higher calling than profits or getting a promotion. A reversion to a "human first" state is called for to help mediate the crisis, and there is no closer a calling to the human state than *doing the right thing.*

How many times in your career or business have you been faced with adversity? It's not a matter of *if* but a matter of *when.* And the way you *react* to what happened is far more important than *what happened* in the first place. We spend so much of our lives fighting what has happened to us both personally and in business that I am afraid we are missing the point if we want to live the principles of The Creator Mindset. Because creatively, it doesn't matter much what happened; all that matters is what you do now. It is far easier to point fingers and blame someone else than it is to move forward in the face of adversity. But I urge you to fight that natural position and instead acknowledge what has happened in your career or business without blaming others or looking for someone to admonish and then move forward and chart a clear path to creativity.

3. COMMUNICATE, COMMUNICATE, COMMUNICATE

Communication is one of those things we often overlook. It's something that most of us feel we do very well even though we don't in our career or company.[7] Often when things go wrong, we are inclined to shut down and wall ourselves off, cutting ourselves off from any communication in order to preserve ourselves.

But the fact is that what is most needed in times like these is not only communication but *over*communication.

In 1982, most communication across the world was done by telephone. This was an era before the Internet or smartphones. Johnson & Johnson did what they could with what they had: the telephone. They set up a toll-free 800 number that anyone could call with questions about the Tylenol scare,[8] and the phone kept ringing. As word was getting out that the tainted Tylenol capsules could be anywhere, folks got scared and wanted answers. Who better to give those answers than the company that made the pills?

Today, there are countless ways to stay connected and communicate, and this becomes paramount when a crisis occurs. But communication today has mostly become completely devoid of human vulnerability and restoration of trust.

The techniques that I teach require you to build communication with the goal of having the largest amount of information available no matter what or how bad the news is. There has to be an honest and direct value to your communication when a crisis occurs so that people can use the information reliably and— here's an important part—*make a decision themselves.* When you use these techniques, you treat people with respect and allow them to make up their own minds. This is no time for cover-ups or half-truths; instead, this is the time to get out all your available tools to reach as many people as possible.

4. CREATE INNOVATION

Crisis can bring about one of the best times possible for creativity. If you follow the first three steps, something amazing will happen. You will generate creative equity in the form of innovation, making lemonade from lemons. In the worst time possible, when all hope seems lost, creativity will shed a light for forward progress.

This is exactly what happened in the Tylenol case. Johnson & Johnson looked at the packaging that was tampered with and instituted new safety measures that are still used today. They asked themselves, What can we do to assure the reliability of the product once it goes out into the marketplace? The answer to that became what is now the industry standard. The glued-shut box, the plastic wrap around the neck of the bottle, and the foil seal over the mouth of the bottle were all the result of creativity at work during a crisis. Today, you can't go into a store and buy a bottle of medicine that lacks these security measures. It says right on the bottle that if the seal is missing, don't buy the product.

The next time you take a seal off any food or drug item, you'll know why the protection was put there in the first place: it was creativity born out of the worst possible situation, and it was creativity that continues to save countless lives.

■   ■   ■

FOLLOWING THE FOUR STEPS of managing crisis can seem counterintuitive at first. It may seem that the last thing you would want to do when you have uncovered a crisis in your career or company would be to allow yourself to become completely and utterly vulnerable or seek and rebuild trust at all costs or communicate across all available channels no matter how bad the news is or allow these things to spur new creativity. That seems extraordinary, but when we view trust as a creative tool across all these techniques, it begins to make more and more sense. What will end up happening with these tools is that your career or business will build honest trust and humility and therefore empathy with your brand. It will allow for healing.

In this case, Johnson & Johnson was the unfortunate victim of a malicious tampering crime. That tampering could have happened to any other company, but the public was able to slowly but surely regain its trust in the brand by the actions the company took. Just two months after the crisis, in November 1982, Tylenol went on to become the nation's favorite pain reliever once again, showing how creativity is one of the best tools to use in a crisis.[9]

sand castle

The Complacency Conundrum

BUSINESSES ALL AROUND the world make stupid assumptions about the future that are based on the past. Leaders think, If the revenue was x last year, then we must be on target to do y next year." Or they might think, We attracted top talent in Q1, so in Q2 we'll continue to attract top talent as well. However, the reality is that if we define success as always growing, developing, reaching new heights, and expanding our footprint in terms of revenue, profit, and transformation, looking at the past is the *last* thing we want to do.

It's amazing how many companies fall into complacency on the basis of the tiniest shred of success. They pat themselves on the back at the smallest bit of accomplishment and then race as fast as possible to do nothing. They choose not to do even one thing that could affect the growth of the company tomorrow. They don't move an inch. Think of Kodak in Chapter 17. They were in the photo business and an employee had an idea to digitize photos, from their own lab no less! But that idea was never taken seriously because the leadership was stuck in the past.

Kodak got it wrong about digital photos. Later in this chapter we will look at a few more case studies of businesses and see where it all went wrong. Perhaps most important, we will discuss what you can learn from their mistakes to make sure they don't occur in your career or business. The common and underlying theme for all the companies in this section is that they got complacent. Complacency has an impact on both creativity and the bottom line. It's truly a castle made of sand, ignoring the tide that is mere inches away. Businesses that are built on lofty assumptions that the world will remain constant and their future success is assured will end up going out of business. Complacency is a one-way ticket to doom, a foolish journey that appears from the outside to be so easy to avoid yet from the inside pulls down some of the giants of industry. We will look at what happens when complacency takes over and creativity dies.

Complacency usually manifests in three distinct flavors:

1. The Early Warning

2. Exploitive Sales

3. Paralysis of Choice

No matter which flavor occurs, when creativity dies in a company or career, its eventual end is soon cast in stone. Let's take a look at three companies that have gone out of business and examine why one of my three distinct flavors of complacency ultimately led to their demise.

A TOY BUSINESS TO LEARN FROM

Toys "R" Us was once a thriving business. Anyone who was a kid in the 1980s and early 1990s can remember that a visit to Toys "R" Us was one of the most special times of childhood. It was a store that was packed with toys of all kinds, with not an inch of empty space. With dolls, video games, bikes, Silly Putty, board games, remote control cars, and just about every other toy imaginable, it was like a fantasy land for kids.

Toys "R" Us was started by Charles Lazarus in 1948 as a baby furniture store. As Lazarus began to add more toys to the store, he found that customers were coming in for the toys, not to buy furniture, and after several years of seeing this trend, he decided to open a dedicated toy store in 1957.[1] He named it Toys "R" Us because he felt that most likely people would understand what he was doing from the get-go, and it worked. At its peak, Toys "R" Us operated 1,500 stores globally, including 900 in the United States.[2]

But soon what worked so well was no longer enough. Why was Toys "R" Us beginning to falter, and what can we learn from this particular case of complacency? Let's take a look.

Complacency Sign 1: The Early Warning

Every career or business change will signal what I call The Early Warning. It is a warning signal of some sort that indicates imminent change. Sometimes the change comes all at once, and sometimes it's a slow-moving mechanism. Yet in all cases an Early Warning signal occurs, and it's your job to see it, listen to it, feel it, and otherwise recognize it.

Toys "R" Us drove the car while looking in the rearview mirror. Behind Toys "R" Us were years and years of growth and a track record of impressive sales that included healthy margins and rosy earnings, but they let this view blind their vision of what was in front of them. They did not perceive The Early Warning that was occurring all around them.

For Toys "R" Us, the first Early Warning was that the Internet was beginning to take shape in the late 1990s. New toy shops were opening up online, including Amazon. Then, by the early 2000s people were buying toys as part of a larger shopping trip to other retailers, such as Walmart and Target.[3] Convenience, not selection, was the norm of the day. People not only had more options but more convenient ones too. Even though Toys "R" Us saw that the sale of toys online was the wave of the future, they did nothing about it because they got complacent. They *chose* to do nothing about The Early Warning happening all around them.

The second Early Warning that Toys "R" Us did not pay attention to was that most retail stores had started moving toward curated experiences. A curated experience is a retail space environment where products can be touched, felt, and experienced firsthand. With the products taken out of the packaging and off the shelf, this is a retail space where products can come to life. At other toy stores, children were able to play with toys and products out of the box, allowing them to push the buttons, play with the toys, and see for themselves if they liked them. Also, other retailers were beginning to make areas for experiences such as superhero zones and storytime hour to create other reasons to be at a store other than a purchase. But Toys "R" Us did none of these things. And eventually Toys "R" Us went out of business for no other reason than that they got complacent and could not read their multiple Early Warnings.

■ ■ ■

WHAT IN YOUR CAREER or business is approaching a shift or change in the way things have always been done? What is your Early Warning? This will be very specific to your career sector or business field, but it is out there to see only if you choose to see it and pay attention.

To pay attention, you must look at what the market is doing and not assume that you are immune. Don't get so comfortable that you cannot see what others are doing. Take a look at your business as a whole and see if there are folks doing things a different way. Is there a shift in some subtleties of how the product or service is being delivered, consumed, or purchased? Even a slight difference can signal an Early Warning. Are people using the product or service in a new and different way?

The comfort of looking to the past for answers is tempting, but to spark creativity, you must move out of yesterday and into tomorrow and look very carefully at what is going on around you. What is directly in front of you signaling The Early Warning of coming change that you can adapt to creatively?

There may be two or three or more Early Warnings that you have to contend with, and here priority is what matters most. If you are able to identify multiple Early Warnings, you must attach a priority to the one that is most likely to occur the soonest and visit the issue with The Creator Mindset tools to unblock progress.

CASE STUDY 2

A SUBSCRIPTION SERVICE TO LEARN FROM

Columbia House was formed in 1955 as the Columbia Record Club to propel the exploding music market in the United States.

It was a business that offered great convenience: you would get several records or, later, CDs or DVDs for mere pennies and automatically receive additional products in the mail monthly. Americans loved nothing more than new music or movies from their favorite artists and actors, and they signed up for the service in droves. No one read the contract; people just wanted a great deal. This growth continued for Columbia House until the late 2000s. At the height of their success in 1996 they had a revenue of $1.4 billion.[4]

But it came at a steep Exploitive Sale cost, and soon things began to falter. Why was Columbia House beginning to falter, and what can we learn from this case of complacency?

Complacency Sign 2: The Exploitive Sale

No one likes to feel exploited when it comes to buying something. No one likes to buy a product or service and feel that he or she is being taken on the proverbial ride. With unfair fees or services, we pay for what we don't need, and it goes on and on. As one of the basic tenets of The Creator Mindset is direct honesty, Exploitive Sales is a topic we need to learn so that we don't get complacent.

Exploitive Sales work, though, and that's why its pull into complacency is so strong. It is a technique that homes in on our weakness as human beings and uses it to get us to purchase a product or service over and over. But it is not sustainable.

In this case, Columbia House was making a significant portion of its revenue from recurring fees that made people feel exploited. Those fees were charged monthly when people signed up to get DVDs or CDs for pennies each and entered a long-term contract to buy more and more. Columbia House's revenue model was based on exploiting the human condition—Exploitive

Sales. In this case, it was exploiting the fact that people are inherently attracted to a deal. Folks have a lot going on in their lives, and convenience and a deal make a winning combo. But making a business model out of recurring charges on contracts that no one ever reads plays on this inherent human condition and is a disaster in any sustainable long-term business plan. Much as some car dealers make more money from financing cars than they do on an initial sale, Columbia House made more money on the long-term contract than it did on any initial sale. Although 12 CDs or DVDs might initially sell for a penny, you would have to sign up to receive a few DVDs or CDs each month at full price for years in some cases.[5]

When you build a business on exploiting human weakness, people are bound to get fed up. Columbia House had a hard time collecting fees from people who were upset. Those people felt trapped. There are legendary stories from that time of folks receiving threatening letters from Columbia House lawyers that sounded scary and referenced contract clauses people hadn't even read.[6] People all over were sick and tired of it. They wanted to listen to music and get a good deal but didn't want to subscribe to a long-term service and each and every month be subject to a fee or charge. Adding insult to injury, if you didn't select the music or movies you wanted by a certain time, they would send you whatever they thought fit and charge you for it. Layer in some fees and service charges for this or that (but it was in the contract!) and you can see how people felt exploited.

What in your career or business is built on the Exploitive Sale? It's time to get serious and take a moment to search deep within ourselves to find what it is that we are using to exploit others with to create an advantage. It's not a comfortable discussion and it may be hard to talk about, but it's a must, because to move forward with creativity, we have to learn to stop or reverse

Exploitive Sales before they lull us into complacency because they are not sustainable and morally they are *just not right*. This is something that you need to do today. Set up a weaning process and move away from Exploitive Sales and into an honest and direct exchange.

What is it that you are doing that captures a buyer and keeps that buyer unwillingly? Is there a technique you are using in your career that you feel only *you* can use and no one else can? Are you building your entire career or business on this Exploitive Sale? Are you using this technique as the only way to move forward?

Part of The Creator Mindset mandates that you continuously innovate and use creativity to grow. You don't need to force someone to do business with you if your business or career is infused with creativity. Things that are inclusive of the human condition and leverage the best of who we are rather than exploit it will always work in the long term. Sooner or later people will get sick and tired of being exploited, and even if it helps your career or business, it is only a short-term gain that is devoid of creativity and mirth.

What ended up happening with Columbia House? Other companies developed subscription services that let people buy music or movies for one low fee that was fully disclosed, with no long-term contract and no Exploitive Sale. That was revolutionary at the time. Services such as iTunes worked this way and were damaging to the Columbia House model. But they weren't nearly as damaging to the Columbia House model as Columbia House was to itself. Because of complacency Columbia House thought, We are the biggest and the best. Screw the customer! That's how we are making money, and if people don't want to subscribe and receive goods each month and pay what we say, they need to live with the consequences.

But again and again, Columbia House got complacent about the Exploitive Sale. Instead of innovating and using creativity to serve a huge customer base and move to a model that was not built on the Exploitive Sale, they got complacent, and soon they went bankrupt. Columbia House went out of business on August 10, 2015, to the great relief of millions worldwide who were still stuck with its contracts.

CASE STUDY 3

AN AIRLINE TO LEARN FROM

Pan American Airways was the largest international carrier in the United States. It started in 1927 hauling mail from Key West to Cuba, pioneered international travel, and by the late 1940s employed 19,000 people in 62 countries.[7] Pan Am grew to become the largest airline in the world until 1969, and its creative innovations were the reason behind its growing success.[8] It was the first airline to make reservations on a computer for both flights and hotels; this happened in 1964, when computers were large enough to take up a full floor of an office building. When this company started, there was creativity running in its veins.

This airline also revolutionized the use of jets, starting with the Boeing 707 in 1958, when almost everyone else was still using propeller aircraft.[9] Jet-powered aircraft then gave Pan Am incredible ingenuity in terms of market share. It was now able to fly to over 160 countries and serve every continent in the world except Antarctica.[10] It owned a chain of hotels and had cash reserves of millions of dollars in the late 1960s. Things were going right, and culturally, the brand touched the hearts and minds of consumers all over the world.

An image of the jet set flying anywhere in the world in the lap of luxury was promoted by Pan Am. It was one of the world's first lifestyle brands. Sure, they flew planes, but what they really did was capture America's yearning for adventure. Pan Am made flying a pleasure for the masses, and all it took to participate was the price of a ticket.

But soon things began to falter. What caused that shift, and what can we learn from this particular case of complacency? Let's find out.

Complacency Sign 3: Paralysis of Choice

Paralysis of Choice is a complacency trap that I define as having too many options and not choosing one to pursue. In failing to choose a route, you become complacent by default. Paralysis of Choice tends to happen to companies and to careers at the *height of their success* (though not always) because things are going so well and so much creativity is being generated that there are many creative options to consider. But these options are not acted on, and complacency takes over. What ends up happening is that the sheer number of options—even if those options are limited to one or two—leaves the employee or company in a Paralysis of Choice: an overwhelmed lack of action.

Pan Am had Paralysis of Choice. When competition for routes and integration in the newly deregulated US market was introduced, Pan Am continued to believe that there was no need to change. The option to participate and compete in the new market was there, but there was a shocking and almost numb reaction to that change. What ended up happening? Nothing. Paralysis of Choice caused Pan Am to do nothing.

Advances in security features were beginning to take hold around the industry after terrorists began to hijack airplanes (many of them Pan Am flights) and kill innocent people. There were companies that scanned baggage, did bag checks, and profiled passengers much as we do today before people board a flight. They had tons of options to enact here and once again claim innovation and creativity leadership, but Pan Am was complacent and did nothing to enact a new security policy.[11] Creativity was the very definition of Pan Am when the company started, but just a few years later, in 1991, Pan Am declared bankruptcy, forever relegated to the history books of aviation.

■ ■ ■

WHAT IN YOUR CAREER or business has you enacting Paralysis of Choice and therefore staying stagnant instead of choosing a road? The decorated Civil War lieutenant general and later president Ulysses S. Grant once said, "Anything is better than indecision. We must decide. If I am wrong, we shall soon find it out and can do the other thing. But not to decide wastes both time and money and may ruin everything."[12]

What other road is in front of you now that leaves you overwhelmed by inaction? What options for a path forward are you generating with creativity and not taking? Moreover, what priority can you assign to these actions? The answer lies in being honest in facing your issues head-on to see what choices you have in front of you and what you can commit to today and then deciding what to leave in and what to leave out.

It is nonsense to think that your market advantage will last forever or that your customer will buy forever. As we have discussed, The Creator Mindset sees nothing but a band of time in which your product or service as it exists today will be consumed by receptive and satisfied customers. No more, no less. It is your job to try to extend this bubble or band of time as long as you can even if it stretches beyond the years of your useful working life. When you use creativity, your product, service, or career becomes far more than just commerce. It becomes a cultural moment, a cultural treasure. It becomes a prized entity near and dear to the hearts of users. Your brand becomes a shepherd of cultural goodwill. And how you use that will, with permission from consumers, is scrutinized by an ever more astute and changing consumer base.

Over and over, attention and time not dedicated to creativity will hasten your demise because a company that does not continuously breed and develop creativity in all that it does is destined to failure. I picked only three companies to profile in this chapter but could have filled entire volumes with case studies of companies that went out of business in those three ways. Complacency and basing assumptions on the past, no matter how they manifest, will crush creativity and soon render your career or company to the past.

Instead, choose creativity to help you deal with these three complacency flavors because at the end of the day, the answer to all forms of complacency is to keep The Creator Mindset growing and vibrant and forever keeping up with change. In this growth and vibrancy there is a chance for a watershed cultural movement that gives your product or service or career—no matter what you do—a chance to become legendary.

sheer panic

Starting Anew

N OW THAT WE have established a guideline for using The Creator Mindset, it's important that we talk about your future outlook on all things involving that mindset.

As a result of reading this book, I hope you now feel that it is time to start anew and make a fresh start on living your Creator Mindset in all that you do: in your business, your career, and your life.

CREATIVITY AND REINVENTION

Mike Ciopyk was a big fan of sports cars. He was just 13 years old in 1972 when he wrote to his favorite German car manufacturer asking for details about an upcoming model.[1] Mike was unlike other boys because he wasn't a fan of BMW or Mercedes, both of which were very popular in the United States at the time. Instead, he was a fan of a less popular manufacturer by the name of Porsche.

Mike wrote to Porsche asking if they would be exporting the 911RS to the United States. It was the race car of his dreams. Amazingly, one day several weeks later a handwritten letter arrived from the Porsche factory in Stuttgart. He tore it open to see that Porsche had replied to him personally, assuring him that yes, the car would be available in the United States and that Porsche would love to have him as a customer when he was old enough.

Today, Mike owns three Porsche cars, achieving what he desired as a teenager. That letter is still a treasured relic of his childhood, but this story is not about Mike. It's about a company that managed to overcome a mistake with reinvention. It was a big, messy, and horrible mistake that is unlike the other examples in this book because it occurred during World War II.

Porsche started as a car company that made vehicles for the Nazis.[2] Ferdinand Porsche, the owner, invented the VW Beetle for Hitler,[3] and under Porsche's parent company, Volkswagen, they had their own concentration camp, Arbeitsdorf, at which prisoners were forced to make cars, tanks, and other vehicles.[4] Their focus at the time was tanks and submersibles, vehicles that would drive the German Army on their conquest of Europe, spreading Nazi ideology far beyond the borders of the home country. But soon the war was over and the Allied forces had won. However, this story is not about the past. It's about the future: How in the world was Porsche able to transcend its history as a car manufacturer that fed the Nazi war machine to the car maker of young Mike Ciopyk's dreams?

The answer lies in reinvention, a revisioning of epic proportions.

Shortly after the war ended, Ferdinand Porsche died, and with him died Porsche's past. Leadership passed to Ferdinand Porsche's son, Ferry, who broke with the past in a hurry. He got creative and decided to direct Porsche's attention to a new and different goal, one that would be able to evolve and stay attuned to changing trends. The company would never make military vehicles again.

The new vision was to make the world's best sport cars and turn the company in a new direction. Ferry knew that this would take time and the best engineering and design. He also knew that it was going to be a tough mountain to climb to get to the same level as their competition, which included Bugatti and Ferrari. But it was a worthwhile goal that was far different from the one that was buried in the ashes of history.

The thing we can learn from Porsche is that no matter what mistakes we have made and no matter how severely wrong we have gotten it in the past, it is possible to learn from the past and move on to a brighter future. Porsche today exists almost entirely in the realm of dreams, a maker of luxurious sports cars with exhilarating performance and engineering. That is an astonishing feat and a far cry from its beginning. It is a reinvention so successful that most people today don't even know how the company started.

In 1999 Porsche decided to finally make amends for its past when it set up a fund to help compensate concentration camp prisoners who were used to build its cars during the war.[5] It also commissioned a study that looked at its past engagements with the Nazi Party and released a comprehensive report.[6] Although those gestures were largely symbolic, today Porsche is laser focused on sports cars, abandoning its earlier roots and replacing them with a modern vision of the reliable sports car.

The Creator Mindset allows for past mistakes to be seeds in the soil of progress. Those seeds end up being the fruit of reinvention, but to get there, you need to have two main components:

1. Break away from the past.

2. Recognize your past.

I know that these may seem somewhat contradictory, but in the end both steps set you on a path toward success and allow you to create the spark of creativity that will enable you to reinvent. Let's take a look at how you can make each one a reality for your business:

1. Break Away from the Past

If you don't like your career's or company's past, change its future. In the case study above, Porsche's postwar vision had nothing to do with its vision during the war. From killing machines to vehicles of sporting pleasure, Porsche literally reinvented itself into a different field. All it took was the will to change paths and break away from the past.

When you break away from the past, your future actions stand on their own merit. They are based not in any historical context but in a context that you deem important. Therefore, if the past is something you would like to change, there is no better way to change it than by changing the future.

Whatever it is that you do, you certainly can determine your future by deciding that you do not want to be defined by your past. It may take a few days, weeks, or years depending on the severity of your history to overcome the stigma of your past, but it is entirely possible if you will it.

Your movement toward this reinvention is dependent on how strongly you desire to change it. Out of the past can come any future you wish.

2. Recognize Your Past

To avoid being defined by the past and succeed in your reinvention, you must recognize your past at some point. Each case is different, but at some time in your reinvention you must recognize where it is that you come from.

Porsche decided in the late 1990s to recognize its past and affirm its roots, but this is not an exact recipe for everyone. Often, recognizing the past needs to happen up front for your reinvention to take hold. But no matter when you do it, recognizing the past helps anchor how far you have come from your original mandate, fully rounding out your transition to reinvention.

■   ■   ■

REINVENTION IS COMPLETELY POSSIBLE and often is a worthwhile goal in pursuing creativity in an ever-changing global environment. Keeping yourself and your company fresh and up to date will become more and more relevant in the future creative economy. Starting on a new path and setting new goals are paramount in your embrace of the principles of The Creator Mindset. As you move away from the stagnant, these two tools will help you shift your path to wherever it is you would like to go, and that is powerful and worthwhile.

CREATIVITY AND THE BIGGER PICTURE

On your road to starting anew with The Creator Mindset, it is imperative that you employ creativity to question the status quo. No matter how widely held a belief is, question everything because The Creator Mindset allows you to look at things differently and in many cases more positively than you have been programmed to do.

We can all agree that we think the world is going to hell in a handbasket, right? I mean, that's what we are exposed to every day. Each time you turn on the TV or check social media, things seem to be going horribly wrong for Mother Earth and her people. Greed is everywhere and is only getting worse. Even charitable giving is suffering because of that greed. Life expectancy is down worldwide as people are dying younger and younger. Pictures of brackish undrinkable water and factories releasing carbon emissions into the air are on autoreplay in our minds.

This negative-only view of the world seems to have been adopted by the majority of people today, but it's not the creative view I seek to impart to you. Instead, I encourage you to challenge the status quo. I uncovered positive news when I looked at these seemingly negative situations through the lens of The Creator Mindset. Take a look.

Life Expectancy Is Increasing for Both Men and Women Worldwide

In Figure 20.1, you see the life expectancy for both men and women blended into one trajectory.[7] It doesn't take a rocket scientist to see that the trajectory goes nowhere but up. Pretty soon people may be living to biblical ages. In 1960, most people died at 53 years of age. Harriette the cavewoman was dead at 30. It takes

FIGURE 20.1

**Average Life Expectancy Worldwide
(Population, Weighted)**

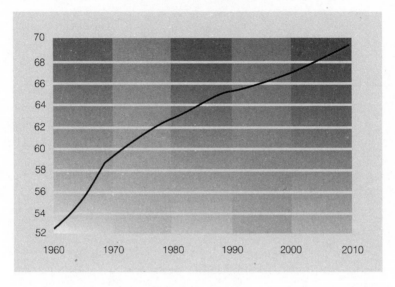

Source: World Bank

creativity to challenge the existing thought system and see beyond the hype and into the light of truth that creativity provides.

Charitable Giving Is Increasing Worldwide, and Americans Are Giving Even More

In Figure 20.2, you can see that giving to charitable organizations is practiced just about everywhere but is especially noteworthy in America.[8] Americans on average give 3 to 15 times more than the residents of other countries in terms of the level of charitable contributions. A recent study found that giving in the United States increases when taxes are reduced.[9] You need to look at things creatively to uncover a more altruistic truth.[10]

FIGURE 20.2

Charitable Giving:
United States versus Other Countries

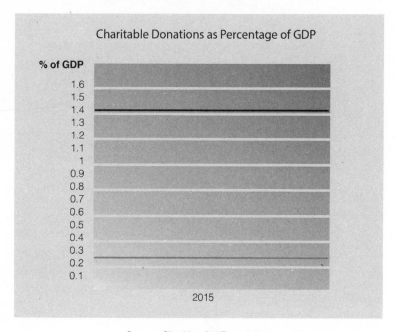

Source: Charities Aid Foundation

Access to Clean Drinking Water Keeps Improving Worldwide

In Figure 20.3, you can see that the number of people who have access to clean drinking water has risen dramatically in the past 25 years.[11] Since 1990, the number of people all over the world who have across to clean, potable drinking water has never been higher, and that is with the population explosion adding roughly 1 billion people every 13 years. All in all, we are doing much better in this area. Yes, there is still a lot to do and we are nowhere near where we want to be and should be, yet the progress we

FIGURE 20.3

Access to Clean Drinking Water Worldwide

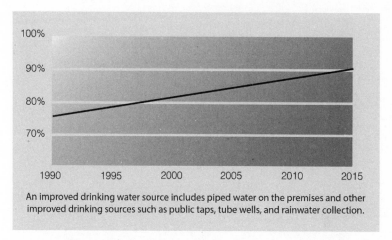

An improved drinking water source includes piped water on the premises and other improved drinking sources such as public taps, tube wells, and rainwater collection.

Source: OurWorldData based on World Bank, World Development Indicators

are making is unmistakable. Even carbon dioxide emissions are down across the United States.[12] All this is remarkable if we fight the pessimism that comes naturally to us and instead look at it in the context of our innate creativity.

■ ■ ■

THROUGH THE LENS OF The Creator Mindset, even widely held beliefs and the ensconced analytical status quo are open to challenge. Creativity releases an eternal light of truth that will shine brightly in all the dark corners of your career, your business, and your world. What will you uncover by looking at your world creatively and challenging established views?

A Closing Note from the Author

THINK IT'S IMPORTANT to look inward at myself and the road I've been on with The Creator Mindset. I thought that good things would last forever, not just in a band of time. I got complacent. I got stuck. I rested on the earliest hint of success. I thought mistakes were to be avoided at all costs. I did not have empathy. I had an inflated ego problem. I was uncaring. I flew off the handle at the slightest provocation from my staff. I made dumb assumptions that were based on the past. I was ignorant of any victory unless it was an epic victory. I talked too much. I was wracked with self-doubt.

I violated every rule in this book, but none was more tragic than this: I lost sight of creativity in favor of the analytical.

The good news is that with The Creator Mindset, you now have the tools to recover from each and every setback and negative situation that you have been faced with or are currently facing. If you do not lose sight of creativity, you will never be left with a problem you cannot solve.

The Creator Mindset is really an everyday practice, not a theoretical approach. Its science is not found in the lab. It's found in your business, your career, and your life. How you apply The Creator Mindset will take on a meaning that will be uniquely yours. It's an important exercise of continuous learning, development, and enrichment that is used day to day in a real-world environment and tweaked continually by the power of creative thought. Something that works today most likely will not work tomorrow, and something that fails today just might be the ticket to tomorrow's success.

It's with these final words that I encourage you to go out and practice The Creator Mindset. I have set up a community where we can all interact and share ideas at www.nirbashan.com /thecreatormindset. I invite you to join me there to continue this dialogue and to keep uncovering creativity and its value to you and your business or career while also continuously developing your ability to solve just about any problem with creativity.

Good luck with your newfound Creator Mindset. Get out there and use your newfound superpower, creator!

Acknowledgments

THIS BOOK WOULD not have been possible without the generous and everlasting patience, guidance, and genius of Jessica Faust. She owns a business called the BookEnds Literary Agency and is one of the most thoughtful people I have met in publishing. She tore into the first 88,000-word manuscript and then told me to throw it away—literally, in the garbage. And that was our first conversation! She asked (forced) me to simplify all the ideas in this book to distill their meaning into an ultrafocused outline that would hold the most value for readers. I will forever be appreciative of her smart approach and understanding of what works for readers and publishers. Wanna do another book, Jessica?

In the same vein, this book would not be possible without Cheryl Segura, my brilliant editor at McGraw Hill Professional. I feel lucky to have worked with her on this title. Talk about vision and steadfast support of this work! Cheryl took the outline I had made with Jessica Faust and gave it real meaning, purpose, clarity, and life. She made me a better writer at every step in the process and helped me find my voice. She is detailed-oriented, smart beyond compare, and disciplined. She also has a great website, withcheryl.com, where she gives real-life personal and professional advice to the masses. Who better to learn from than a person who edits a plethora of books? On top of that, she found this book to champion in a sea of competitive offers from other publishers, and for that I am thankful and forever grateful.

Donya Dickerson, who is the associate publisher at McGraw Hill Professional—what can I say? You are a rock star. First you hired Cheryl. So nice job there. Then your work ethic and reputation in the publishing business are second to none. Thank you for all you and your staff have done. Nora Hennick, Daina Penikas, and Amanda Muller at McGraw Hill Professional have been wonderful as well as copyeditor Eric Lowenkron. Finally, Mauna Eichner and Lee Fukui, you both are supergifted and talented. You have crafted this book to look amazing, and to you I am grateful.

My fact checker and researcher Bob Dirig worked on this book to check each fact and figure and painstakingly research it and make sure it came from a proper source. He used to be my boss. I worked at a department of archives (yet another job) where he was the chief archivist. He showed me nothing but kindness while I was in his employ. I got to learn a whole lot from him about archives and library science, but what I really learned was how to lead with honesty, conviction, and a love of country and western music. Bob was invaluable throughout the process of putting this book together, running fact-checking missions all over the place, and I am indebted to him for his work on this book. See you in the stacks, sir.

Speaking of stacks, the ArtCenter College of Design in Pasadena opened its impressive library to me and Bob Dirig, as did the Los Angeles County Library, the Los Angeles Public Library, the Pasadena City College Library, and the Pasadena Public Library. Frank Jung, who is the director of the Porsche Historical Archives, and Jens Torner, who manages the photo archive for Porsche, were instrumental in their help with the research out of Zuffenhausen, Germany.

Michael Morsberger, Ken Schmidt, Brig. Gen Thomas Kolditz, Jae Goodman, Anthony Reeves, Dr. John Whyte, AJ Jacobs, Marcus Collins, Emily Balcetis, Mark C. Thompson, Kerstin

Emhoff, Douglas P. Wickert, Caroline Johnson, Adam Alter, Amy C. Edmondson, Allen Gannett, Lorraine Justice, Richard Turrin, Gordon Tredgold, Ajay Agrawal, John Biggs, Wayne Baker, J.F. Musial, Dr. John Scherer, Mike Wolfsohn, Lisa Bodell, Brian Solis, Alina Wheeler, Mike Covert, Donald Robertson, Chris Griffiths, Srinivas Rao, Heather E. McGowan, David J. Bland, Nicole Srock Stanley, Fran Luckin, Sean Buckley, Jason Sperling, Norm Brady, Kimberly Friedmutter, David Zinger, Barry Brockway, Dale Moore, Toby Daniels, Don McNeill, Scott Goodson, Scott Saunders, Stephen Shapiro, Tim Maleeny, Marshall Goldsmith, Jonah Berger, Nir Eyal, William C. Taylor, Greg McKeown and General Stanley McChrystal all dedicated their time and effort to reading the manuscript ahead of time and providing endorsements, thoughts, and ideas, and for this I am forever grateful and appreciative.

Dr. Ken Alexander is a fantastic human being who cares more about children than just about anyone I have ever met. He served as a general medical researcher and fact checker for this book. His selfless dedication to the eradication of childhood disease and his mission to immunize should stand as an inspiration to his colleagues and to the world of pediatric medicine. He worked tirelessly on this manuscript, going over every detail that had to do with medicine, and recommended changes to this body of work that only made it stronger. I feel lucky to be counted among his friends. Dr. Beth Colleen Long, who is chief of behavioral health in pediatrics at a prestigious children's hospital, has been indispensable in her help on creativity in the developing minds of children. Her help on this project and introduction to creative testing methods made this manuscript stronger. Dr. Robert Bilder offered great help on how the brain processes creativity and the age-old nature versus nurture aspect of learning creativity, and for that I am grateful.

Sean Larson is a good man and a very skilled lawyer. He and the rest of the legal team at HK Law in Cheyenne, Wyoming, do a great job each and every time and helped on this book in innumerable ways. To Robert Solomon a great big thank you for the help you have given me while consulting on the book even if you didn't feel like you helped! Daniel James Walker has been a very helpful supporter of this project from the start. His expertise in video editing, compositing, and VFX is second to none, and for that I am filled with gratitude. David Ratner helped with all the PR-related work around this book, and to him and his team I am grateful for their expertise and thoughtful approach.

Ish Orbegon, Jeff Chean, and Jim Wojo—you guys have always been a source of inspiration and fresh thinking, and your accomplishments over the years have been profound and helped shape this book. Bob Peterson, you were a key mentor in shaping my vision over the years, and I am forever grateful to you and Kathy for being great people and helping out in any way possible with this title. Meghan Driscoll has provided the chapter character art along with Rebecca Berrington, who provided the hand-drawn typeface and a few of the characters as well. I am grateful to the both of you! You have made sections of the book come to life in humorous, interesting, and engaging ways.

Juliet Dayday, F. Pakko De La Torre-Rocha, Armando Ceron, Slava Morshch, Vidur Raswant, John Payne, Rob Siltanen, Joe Hemp, David Angelo, John Boiler, Claude and Gary McDonald, Scott McCollum, Geoff McGann, Jessica Stehlin, Marcus Wesson, Josianne Cote, Jason Johnson, Josh Lieber, Canice Neary, Mike Wolfsohn, Paul Drury, Warren Quan, Jason Sperling, Greg Miller, Cliff Ryder, Peter Ruthenberg, Z. Gevorkian, Pat Wynne, Kevin May, Jim Kiriakakis, Sean Buckley, Chloe Corwin, and many others I am not intentionally leaving out—you have touched my life and this book in amazing and lasting ways, and I am forever grateful for having known each and every one of you.

Kekai Beyer, I want to thank you for dealing with my annoying phone calls, texts, and conversations drilling into the details of this book. I'm sure that by the 100th conversation about Chapter 6 you were done hearing about it, but no, you have shown sagelike patience, advice, and support. You have believed in any creative idea I ever had and have acted as a sounding board for all things creativity. You have been my best friend for decades and your support over the years has been never-ending, and for that you have my everlasting and deepest appreciation.

My brother Nadav Bashan has taught me more than I ever learned in school about leadership and creativity. Real-world leadership is an ability to amass trust from staff, and Nadav has a natural ability to get anyone to go into battle fearlessly. He has taught me about the human element of leadership in countless ways, and I am grateful for his mentorship, support, friendship, and help on this book. Hana and Ram, my parents, and Yaniv Bashan, my brother, have been with me on each step of this journey, and I am indebted for their everlasting support.

My wife, Marisa, has been very patient and understanding with me over the process of putting this book together and the many years it took to complete it. For all the nights, weekends, and precious free hours here and there while this book was coming together, she has acted as an ongoing consultant and coach for both our lives and this project. Your thoughts are always smart, your feedback laser-focused, and your sense of humor glorious. You have helped on this book in untold ways and shaped me to be better at every step with your wisdom.

Finally, to my son Jacob. I am truly blessed to have you in my life. Everything else pales in comparison to the love I have for you, which started the moment I held you in my arms just minutes after you were born. That love will stand the rest of time.

Notes

Introduction

1. U.S. Bureau of Labor Statistics, "Entrepreneurship and the U.S. Economy." Last modified April 28, 2016. https://www.bls.gov/bdm/entrepreneur ship/bdm_chart3.htm.

Chapter 1

1. Sandro Galea, "Mental Health Should Matter as Much as Physical Health, *Psychology Today*, March 25, 2019, https://www.psychologytoday.com /us/blog/talking-about-health/201903/mental-health-should-matter -much-physical-health.
2. James Lake, "Urgent Need for Improved Mental Health Care and a More Collaborative Model of Care," *Permanente Journal*, 21 (2017).
3. Tim Newman, "The Neuroscience of Creativity," *Medical News Today*, February 17, 2016, https://www.medicalnewstoday.com/articles/306 611.php.
4. R. Siva Kumar, "Animals Are Creative Like Humans, But Do Not Take It Forward," *Science Times*, April 25, 2017, https://www.sciencetimes .com/articles/13424/20170425/animals-creative-humans-sonnets.htm.
5. In one example, as described by Normal Doidge, MD, a man who lost his sight as an adult as a result of an autoimmune condition in the eyes was able through neuroplastic exercises to rewire his visual system and see again. Norman Doidge, *The Brain's Way of Healing: Remarkable Discoveries and Recoveries from the Frontiers of Neuroplasticity* (New York: Viking, 2015).
6. Bryan Kolb and Arif Muhammad, "Harnessing the Power of Neuro-plasticity for Intervention," *Frontiers in Human Neuroscience*, June 27, 2014, https://www.frontiersin.org/articles/10.3389/fnhum.2014.00377 /full.
7. Michael Rugnetta, "Neuroplasticty," Encyclopedia Britannica. https:// www.britannica.com/science/neuroplasticity. Updated March 28, 2019.
8. Theodor Herzl, *The Old New Land* (Leipzig, Germany: Hermann See-mann Nachfolger, 1902).

9. The Messerli Research Institute in Vienna did a study with older dogs using touchscreen tables. Their argument was that even though older dogs may not be as physically able to be trained, they can do cognitive problem solving, which will keep them mentally fit. See Amanda Carrozza, "You Can—and Should—Teach Old Dogs New Tricks," *American Veterinarian*, February 16, 2018, https://www.americanveterinarian.com /news/you-canand-shouldteach-old-dogs-new-tricks.

10. Nicholas Carr, *The Shallows: What the Internet Is Doing to Our Brains* (New York: Norton, 2011), 26.

11. Edythe McNamee and Jacque Wilson, "A Nobel Prize with Help from Sea Slugs," CNN.com, May 14, 2013, https://www.cnn.com/2013 /05/14/health/lifeswork-eric-kandel-memory/index.html.

12. Eric Haseltine uses the example of "functional fixedness," something people develop that prohibits creativity. He presents an example of someone wanting to make pancakes but not having a mixer. Instead, that person uses a drill and a pair of scissors. Our analytical brains see only the common functions of those tools, but by "quieting" that side of brain and enhancing the creative side, we can envision different mechanisms that would work as a mixer. See Eric Haseltine, "7 Extraordinary Feats Your Brain Can Perform," *Psychology Today*, November 2018, 54–63.

13. Franz Röösli, Michael Sontag, and Doug Kirkpatrick, "Management Plasticity: Neuronal Networking as the Organizing Principle for Enterprise Architecture to Unfold Human Potential and Creativity," *Challenging Organizations and Society: Reflective Hybrids (COS)*, 4:1 (2015): 684–736. Accessed June 4, 2019. https://www.cos-collective.com/cms /wp-content/uploads/COS_2015_Volume_4_Issue_1_Management _Plasticity-1.pdf. The authors propose that organizations can facilitate neuroplasticity by retraining the way the brain understands traditional organizational structures and practices, allowing for creative solutions to improve business. The authors define this as "management plasticity," meaning "the ability of organizational management to engage the energy and potential of each member to collaboratively, creatively and effectively learn from and adapt to dynamic internal or external changes, opportunities or threats."

Chapter 2

1. Cathy Booth, "Steve's Job: Restart Apple," *Time*, August 1997, 28–34.

2. Mat Honan, "Remembering the Apple Newton's Prophetic Failure and Lasting Impact," *Wired*, August 5, 2013, https://www.wired .com/2013/08/remembering-the-apple-newtons-prophetic-failure-and -lasting-ideals/.

3. Doron P. Levin, "Grim Outlook of Early 1980's Is Back for U.S. Auto Makers," *New York Times*, December 7, 1989, https://www.nytimes.com/1989/12/07/business/grim-outlook-of-early-1980-s-is-back-for-us-auto-makers.html.

4. Lawrence M. Fisher, "Apple Plans 1,300 Layoffs and Takes Loss," *New York Times*, January 18, 1996.

5. Booth, op cit.

6. For more information on the Apple deal with Microsoft, see Booth, op cit., and Walter Isaacson, *Steve Jobs* (New York: Simon & Schuster, 2011), 323–326.

Chapter 3

1. Sandra W. Russ, "Play and Creativity: Developmental Issues," *Scandinavian Journal of Educational Research* 47(3), (2010): 291–303.

2. Adele Diamond, "Development of Cognitive Functions Is Linked to the Prefrontal Cortex," in *The Role of Early Experience in Infant Development*, ed. Nathan A. Fox, Lewis A. Leavitt, and John G. Warhol (Johnson & Johnson Consumer Companies), 131–133. Diamond presents an example of how infants become creative problem solvers when they are around 8.5 to 9 months old. A toy is placed in a transparent box with one side open. Infants age six to eight months tried to put their hands straight through the box from the point where they were looking to reach the toy, but slightly older infants knew to reposition their arms around the box to reach the opening.

3. Amanda Habermann, "Why We Resist Change," *Psychology Today*, January 25, 2017, https://www.psychologytoday.com/us/blog/the-truisms-wellness/201701/why-we-resist-change.

Chapter 5

1. Although some companies and individuals had tested AI in the early 1950s, the birth of AI research is often credited to the Dartmouth Summer Research Project in 1956, which was proposed by individuals at Dartmouth College, Harvard University, IBM, and Bell Telephone Laboratories. See James Moor, "The Dartmouth College Artificial Intelligence Conference: The Next Fifty Years," *AI Magazine* 27, 4 (2006)4, https://pdfs.semanticscholar.org/d486/9863b5da0fa4ff5707fa972c6e1dc92474f6.pdf, and "Artificial Intelligence (AI) Coined at Dartmouth," Dartmouth College 250th anniversary website, accessed August 4, 2019, https://250.dartmouth.edu/highlights/artificial-intelligence-ai-coined-dartmouth.

2. Liqun Luo, "Why Is the Human Brian So Efficient?" *Nautilus*, April 12, 2018, http://nautil.us/issue/59/connections/why-is-the-human-brain-so-efficient.

3. Jennifer Kite-Powell, "How Do We Create Artificial Intelligence That Is More Human?" *Forbes*, March 19, 2019, https://www.forbes.com/sites /jenniferhicks/2019/03/19/how-do-we-create-artificial-intelligence-that -is-more-human/#1eff8b811492.

4. Peter Sarnoff, "A New Amazon Patent Reveals Alexa Could Become Emotionally Intelligent," *Business Insider*, October 17, 2018, https:// www.businessinsider.com/amazon-patent-alexa-emotional-intelligence -2018-10.

Chapter 6

1. Helen Briggs, "Did Our Ancient Ancestors 'Kill the Cat'?" *BBC News*, December 2, 2015, https://www.bbc.com/news/science-environment -34944560.

2. Sindya N. Bhanoo, "Life Span of Early Man Same as Neanderthals'," *New York Times*, January 10, 2011, https://www.nytimes.com /2011/01/11/science/11obneanderthal.html.

3. Steven Mithen, *Problem-Solving and the Evolution of Human Culture*, Monograph Series No. 33 (London: Institute for Cultural Research, 1999), http://citeseerx.ist.psu.edu/viewdoc/download?doi=10.1.1.520 .2184&rep=rep1&type=pdf.

4. "History of Salk," accessed August 9, 2019, https://www.salk.edu /about/history-of-salk/jonas-salk/.

5. Drake Baer, "The Making of Tesla: Invention, Betrayal, and the Birth of the Roadster," *Business Insider*, November 11, 2014, https://www .businessinsider.com/tesla-the-origin-story-2014-10.

6. Jim Taylor, "Is Our Survival Instinct Failing Us?" *Psychology Today*, June 12, 2012, https://www.psychologytoday.com/us/blog/the-power -prime/201206/is-our-survival-instinct-failing-us.

Chapter 7

1. Yogendra Kumar Gupta, Meenakshi Meenu, and Prafull Mohan, "The Tamiflu Fiasco and Lessons Learnt," *Indian Journal of Pharmacology*, 47, 1 (2015): 11–16, https://www.ncbi.nlm.nih.gov/pmc/articles /PMC4375804/.

2. Nancy Colier, "Why Negative Thinking Is Such a Dangerous Habit," *Psychology Today*, April 15, 2019, https://www.psychologytoday.com /us/blog/inviting-monkey-tea/201904/why-negative-thinking-is-such -dangerous-habit.

Chapter 9

1. "How Managers Are Killing Productivity with Useless Meetings That Cost $37 Billion/Year," *Digital Synopsis*, accessed March 6, 2020, https://digitalsynopsis.com/tools/meetings-are-a-waste-of-time/.

2. Sophia Epstein, "Meetings Are a Total Waste of Time: Here's How to Make Them Useful," *Wired*, December 2, 2019, https://www.wired.co.uk/article/how-to-make-meetings-productive.

3. Ronald B. Adler, George Rodman, and Carrie Cropley Hutchinson, *Understanding Human Communication*, 11th ed., (Oxford and New York: Oxford University Press, 2011), https://global.oup.com/us/companion.websites/9780199747382/student/chapter5/.

Chapter 10

1. Ray Kroc and Robert Anderson, *Grinding it Out: The Making of McDonald's* (Chicago: Henry Regnery, 1977), 5–11.

Chapter 11

1. "Adolf Hitler," History.com, updated May 28, 2019, https://www.history.com/topics/world-war-ii/adolf-hitler-1.

2. *The Discovery and Development of Penicillin, 1928–1945* (London: Alexander Fleming Laboratory Museum, 1999).

3. Ibid.

4. Joseph Henry, *Scientific Writings of Joseph Henry* (Washington: Smithsonian Institution, 1886).

5. "Who Invented Sticky Notes?" *Wonderopolis*, accessed April 20, 2020, https://www.wonderopolis.org/wonder/who-invented-sticky-notes.

6. Barbara Bouffard, "Inventor of the Month—Who Is Edouard Benedictus?" *Innovate Product Design*, November 12, 2013, https://innovate-design.com/inventor-month-edouard-benedictus/.

7. Sam Roberts, "Overlooked No More: Ruth Wakefield, Who Invented the Chocolate Chip Cookie," *New York Times*, accessed March 6, 2020, https://www.nytimes.com/2018/03/21/obituaries/overlooked-ruth-wakefield.html.

Chapter 15

1. Joseph Mazar, Yujia Li, Amy Rosado, Peter Phelan, Kritika Kedarinath, Griffith D. Parks, et al., "Zika Virus as an Oncolytic Treatment of Human Neuroblastoma Cells Requires CD24," *PLOS One*, 13, 7 (July 25, 2018), e0200358. https://doi.org/10.1371/journal.pone.0200358.

2. Joel Rose, "How to Break Free of Our 19th-Century Factory-Model Education System," *The Atlantic*, May 9, 2012, https://www.theatlantic.com/business/archive/2012/05/how-to-break-free-of-our-19th-century-factory-model-education-system/256881/.

Chapter 16

1. Nitasha Tiku, "The WIRED Guide to Internet Addiction," *Wired*, April 18, 2018, https://www.wired.com/story/wired-guide-to-internet-addiction/.

Chapter 17

1. James Estrin, "Kodak's First Digital Moment," *New York Times*, August 12, 2015, https://lens.blogs.nytimes.com/2015/08/12/kodaks-first-digital-moment/?auth=login-email.

2. John Aldred, "The World's First Digital Camera, Introduced by the Man Who Invented It," *DIY Photography*, August 2, 2016, https://www.diy photography.net/worlds-first-digital-camera-introduced-man-invented/.

3. Ibid.

Chapter 18

1. Howard Markel, "How the Tylenol Murders of 1982 Changed the Way We Consume Medication," *PBS News Hour*, accessed June 23, 2019, https://www.pbs.org/newshour/health/tylenol-murders-1982.

2. Sara Olkon, "Tylenol Incident 'Never Goes Away' for Family That Lost 3," *Chicago Tribune*, February 6, 2009, https://www.chicagotribune.com/news/chi-tylenol-janus-06-feb06-story.html.

3. Ed Baumann and John O'Brien, "Getting Away with Murder," *Chicago Tribune*, April 21, 1991, https://www.chicagotribune.com/news/ct-xpm-1991-04-21-9102050598-story.html.

4. During the two years preceding the incident, Johnson & Johnson's stock price rose from the low 20s to 46 1/8 the night before the poisonings. See Thomas Moore, "The Fight to Save Tylenol," *Fortune*, October 7, 1982, https://fortune.com/2012/10/07/the-fight-to-save-tylenol-fortune-1982/.

5. Judith Rehak, "Tylenol Made a Hero Out of Johnson & Johnson: The Recall That Started Them All," *New York Times*, March 23, 2002, https://www.nytimes.com/2002/03/23/your-money/IHT-tylenol-made-a-hero-of-johnson-johnson-the-recall-that-started.html.

6. N. R. Kleinfield, "Tylenol's Rapid Comeback," *New York Times*, September 17, 1983, https://www.nytimes.com/1983/09/17/business/tylenol-s-rapid-comeback.html.

7. IESE Business School, "Why Communication in Companies Is So Poor (and How to Get It Right)," *Forbes*, March 21, 2016, https://www.forbes.com/sites/iese/2016/03/21/why-communication-in-companies-is-so-poor-and-how-to-get-it-right/#7ea50c025ed6.

8. Steven Fink, "The Johnson & Johnson/Tylenol Crisis," in *Crisis Management: Planning for the Inevitable* (New York: AMAZON, 1986), 216.

9. Howard Markel, "How the Tylenol Murders of 1982 Changed the Way We Consume Medication," PBS News Hour, accessed June 23, 2019, https://www.pbs.org/newshour/health/tylenol-murders-1982.

Chapter 19

1. Michael Corkery, "Charles P. Lazarus, Toys 'R' Us Founder, Dies at 94," *New York Times*, March 22, 2018, https://www.nytimes.com/2018/03/22/obituaries/charles-p-lazarus-toys-r-us-founder-dies-at-94.html.
2. Susan Berfield, Eliza Ronalds-Hannon, Matthew Townsend, and Lauren Coleman-Lochner, "Tears 'R' Us: The World's Biggest Toy Store Didn't Have to Die," *Bloomberg Businessweek*, June 6, 2018, https://www.bloomberg.com/news/features/2018-06-06/toys-r-us-the-world-s-biggest-toy-store-didn-t-have-to-die.
3. "What Went Wrong: The Demise of Toys R Us," *Knowledge @ Wharton*, March 14, 2018, https://knowledge.wharton.upenn.edu/article/the-demise-of-toys-r-us/.
4. Laura Wagner, "'8 CDs for a Penny' Company Files for Bankruptcy," *NPR The Two Way*, August 11, 2015, https://www.npr.org/sections/thetwo-way/2015/08/11/431547925/8-cds-for-a-penny-company-files-for-bankruptcy.
5. Ibid.
6. Jack Hamilton, "Columbia House Offered Eight CDs for a Penny, but Its Life Lessons Were Priceless," Slate.com, August 12, 2015, https://slate.com/culture/2015/08/columbia-house-bankrupt-mail-order-cd-clubs-owner-finally-going-out-of-business.html.
7. University of Miami Libraries, "A Brief History of Pan Am," *Cleared to Land: The Records of the Pan American World Airways*, accessed March 6, 2020, http://scholar.library.miami.edu/digital/exhibits/show/panamerican/history.
8. Barnaby Conrad III and Tom Morgan, *Pan Am: An Aviation Legend* (San Francisco: Council Oak Books, 2013), 17.
9. Michael Lombardi, "Seventh Heaven," *Boeing Frontiers*, July 2008, http://www.boeing.com/news/frontiers/archive/2008/july/i_history.pdf.
10. Conrad and Morgan, op cit.
11. John H. Cushman, Jr., "U.S. Panel Is Told of Pan Am Security Flaws," *New York Times*, April 5, 1990, https://www.nytimes.com/1990/04/05/world/us-panel-is-told-of-pan-am-security-flaws.html.
12. Ron Chernow, *Grant* (New York: Penguin Press, 2017), 330.

Chapter 20

1. Mike Ciopyk, letter to the editor, *Porsche Panorama*, June 2019.
2. Ofer Aderet, "Details of Porsche's Nazi Ties Spoil Centennial Bash," *Haaretz*, November 10, 2009, https://www.haaretz.com/israel-news/culture/1.5348608.

3. "Volkswagen," *Holocaust Encyclopedia*, accessed August 2, 2019, https://encyclopedia.ushmm.org/content/en/article/volkswagen-1.
4. Ibid.
5. Aderet, op cit.
6. Wolfram Pyta, Nils Havemann, and Jutta Braun, *Porsche: From Engineering Office to Global Brand* (Munich: Siedler, 2017).
7. World Bank, "Life Expectancy at Birth, Total (Years)," https://data.worldbank.org/indicator/SP.DYN.LE00.IN.
8. The chart is based on data collected between 2007 and 2015 from 24 countries. An average of the countries apart from the United States was used to determine the value for other countries. See Charities Aid Foundation, *Gross Domestic Philanthropy: An International Analysis of GDP, Tax, and Giving*, January 2016.
9. William Freehand, Ben Wilterdink, and Jonathan Williams, "The Effect of State Taxes on Charitable Giving," *The State Factor*, September 2015.
10. Giving USA 2017, "Total Charitable Donations Rise to New High of $390.05 Billion," https://givingusa.org/giving-usa-2017-total-charitable-donations-rise-to-new-high-of-390-05-billion/.
11. Our World in Data, "Share of the Population with Access to Improved Drinking Water, 2015," accessed August 22, 2019, https://ourworldindata.org/grapher/share-of-the-population-with-access-to-improved-drinking-water.
12. U.S. Energy Information Administration, "U.S. Energy-Related Carbon Dioxide Emissions, 2005–2016," February 27, 2019, https://www.eia.gov/environment/emissions/state/analysis/.

A Note on the Type

1. "In Honor of the 100th Birthday of Jan Tschichold," *Font Magazine*, accessed April 21, 2020, https://www.linotype.com/794-12597/return-to-switzerland.html.
2. Ibid.
3. "Jan Tschichold, 1902–1974," *Visual Visionaries*, accessed April 21, 2020, https://design.cmu.edu/sites/default/files/book_rnd_6.pdf.
4. Martin McClellan, "Tschichold, Nazis and Allen Lane: The Modernist Politics of Type," *McSweeney's*, January 27, 2010, https://www.mcsweeneys.net/articles/tschichold-nazis-and-allen-lane-the-modernist-politics-of-type.
5. *Font Magazine*, op cit.
6. Jan Tschichold, "Clay in a Potter's Hand," in *The Form of the Book: Essays on the Morality of Good Design* (Point Roberts, WA: Hartley & Marks, 1991).

Index

A

Actionable plan
  positive thinking for, 55
  results and, 135
  self-doubt preventing, 117–118
Alexander, Kenneth, 118–119
Amazon, 160
Analytical thinking
  Apple with, 11
  artificial intelligence with, 42
  brain and, 38
  business teaching, x, 39–40
  as challenged, 177
  creative shutting out, 33, 48–49
  creative thinking alternated
    with, 7
  creativity and, 22
  creativity lost for, 179
  creativity united with, 23, 37–38
  differences shunned by, 118
  education and, 120–121
  education emphasizing, 39
  failure and, 12
  on multitasking, 131–132
  on one target, 81
  on overload, ix, 8–9
  problem solving and, x, 51–52
  on product, 111
  on profit, 39, 112–113, 157
  quantification for, 39
  self-doubt in, 120–121, 125

Apple
  analytical thinking at, 11
  Microsoft and, 13–14
  stagnation at, 12
  technology from, 11–15, 49
Art
  creativity and, 91–92
  sense subcategories of, 92
Artificial intelligence
  without human attributes, 43
  analytical processing from, 42

B

Bénédictus, Edouard, 88
Blame
  business regulation and,
    100–101
  inflated ego and, 97
  trust without, 152
BMW, 169–170
Brains
  anatomy of, 38
  correction for, 8–9
  neuroplasticity and changing, 5
  new ways for, 8
Break away, 172
Bugatti, 171
Burke, James E., 149, 151
Business
  analytical thinking taught by, x,
    39–40

Business *(cont'd)*
  blame and regulation of,
    100–101
  comfort avoidance for, 102
  complacency by, 157–158
  creativity for, ix–xi, 10
  education from, 62
  on emotional intelligence, 40
  highest-level view of, 27–28
  ideas, concepts, execution for,
    30–31
  inflated ego and death of, 98
  root problem in, 51–52
  yes in, 140

C
Carbon dioxide emissions, 177
CCD. *See* Charged couple device
Challenge
  on analytical thinking, 177
  creative thinking on, 142–143
  solutions pushed by, 85, 139
Change
  in concept, 33–34
  as constant, 11
  creativity hope in, 98
  early warning on, 159, 161
  from ideas, 143
  inflated ego versus, 95
  Pan Am on, 166–167
  as threat, 22
  time guaranteeing, 144
  from will power, 7–8
  yes to, 140
Character, xii
  bad times showing, 99
Charged couple device (CCD), 137
Charitable giving, 175–176
Chean, Jeff, 61–62
Children
  community as, 139–140
  failure and thinking like, 139

  imagination and, 18
  as problem solvers, 18, 21
Ciopyk, Mike, 169–170
Clean drinking water, 176–177
Columbia House, 145
  exploitive sales and, 161–165
Comfort
  business avoiding, 102
  for complacency, 127
  limits on, xiii
  as mistake, 127
  pushed out of, 144–145
  results not from, 102
  self-doubt from, 119–120
  technology for, 128
  uncomfortable and, 133–134
Communication
  in crisis, 152–153
  inflated ego breaking, 98
  process for, 109
  as product, 27, 111
  value provided in, 153
Community
  benefits for, 114
  child thinking as, 139–140
  self-doubt overcome for, 125
  website for, 180
Companies
  analytical strategies by, 12
  creativity for, ix–xi, 10
  ideas for, 3–4
  services packaged for, 9–10
Competition
  as good, 13–14
  listening to, 66–67
  for Pan Am, 166
  for Porsche, 171
Complacency
  by business, 157–158
  comfort for, 127
  conundrum of, xiii
  exploitive sales for, 158, 162

by Pan Am Airlines, 166
past and, 168
stuck in, 179
types of, 158
Computers. *See also*
  Technology
  without creativity, 42–43
  Apple and, 11–15, 49
  Apple and Microsoft in, 13–14
  human mind as, 38–39
  multitasking and, 127–135
  Pan Am with, 165
Concept
  business needing, 30–31
  exercise for, 28
  for pizza restaurant, 31
  radical changes in, 33–34
  Trinity of Creativity as, 26, 31,
    34
  as widest view, 27–28
Connections
  from creative thinking, 135
  creativity and, xv, 43
  creativity for intimate, 49
  empathy as, 65
  humor for, 64
  vulnerability creating, 150
Control
  of approach, 72, 109–110
  humor on, 63
  idea killed by, 53
  of inflated ego, 94, 96
  listening versus, 75
  as mistake, 88, 102
  of self-doubt, 117
  vulnerability versus, 150
Costs, xiv, 22, 71, 141
  cutting of, 12
  of exploitive sale, 162
  of trust restored, 151–155
Could be, 18, 102–103
  creative mind seeing, xvi, 86

Courage, xii, 86
  for creativity, 62
  as difficult, 68–69
  as listening, 68
  new actions as, 67
  problems overcome by, 62
  self belief as, 68
Creative idea economy, xiv, 16
  innovation in, 153–154
  reinvention for, 173
Creative thinking
  analytical alternated with, 7
  analytical shut out by, 33, 48–49
  on boundaries, 142–143
  brain and, 38
  connections from, 135
  "could be" seen by, xvi, 86
  doubt of, 39
  Jobs and, 13–14
  on product, 111–112
  on root problem, 52–53
  for tweaking, 179–180
  as underdeveloped, ix, 8
Creativity
  through analytical barriers, 22
  alternatives popping as, 32
  analytical and lost, 179
  analytical united with, 23, 37–38
  art as subset and, 91–92
  as being yourself, 100
  for business, ix–xi, 10
  calculated risk of, 15
  change and hope for, 98
  for companies, ix–xi, 10
  computers without, 42–43
  connection through, xv, 43
  as ego antidote, 96
  emotional intelligence from, 40
  exercise for, 41–42
  failure from lack of, 168
  from focus, 133
  fostering of, 92–93

Creativity *(cont'd)*
  growth for, 105–106
  harmonic theory on, 134–135
  for human attributes, 49
  human element exercise for,
    43–44
  humor, empathy, courage for, 62
  humor sparking, 63–64
  imagination captured by, 48
  imperfection loved boosting, 87
  inflated ego shutting, 94, 98
  as innovation, 93
  intimate connection from, 49
  as learned, 5
  from little victory, 81
  logic with, 6–7
  mind wandering in, 32–33
  from mistakes, 83–84
  moved by, 14–15
  natural instincts versus, 102–103
  from necessity, 45–47
  norms questioned and, 101–102
  paralysis of choice and, 166
  personality traits of, xii
  with positive thinking, 52–54
  as possibility, 17–18
  potential seen by, 103
  for problem solving, x, xv,
    38–39
  process with, 109
  on profit, 93, 112–114
  questions for, 72
  as seeing differently, xvi, 44
  solutions by, 93
  spread of, 47–48
  as taught, 20, 25–26
  as tool, 5–6
  from uncomfortable, 134
  as variations, 33–34
Crisis
  four steps for, 147–155
  guide for, xiii

Croc, Ray, 80–81

D
Detox day, 129
Digital camera, 138
Disruption, 140
Drawing exercise, 19

E
Early warning
  on change, 159, 161
  on complacency, 158
Education, 17
  analytical thinking in, 39
  from boss, 62
  for creativity, 5, 20, 25–26
  by fear, 142
  guesses not part of, 121
  right answers in, 120–121
Ego, xii
  apology and weight of, 97–98
  blame and inflated, 97
  business death and inflated, 98
  change versus inflated, 95
  communication and, 98
  control of inflated, 94, 96
  creativity and inflated, 94, 98
  creativity as antidote and, 96
  failure and inflated, 96
  ineffective leadership and, 96
  inflation of, 93–94, 179
  self and, 32–33, 68, 100
  as self-worth, 93
  success for inflated, 94–95
Emotional intelligence
  business on, 40
  creativity growing, 40
  empathy in, xii, 62, 64–67, 86,
    179
  hiring and, 40
  human element in, 44
Empathy, xii, 86

as connections, 65
for creativity, 62
as external, 64, 66–67
as internal, 64–66
judgment opposite of, 66–67
as listening, 65–66
problems overcome by, 62
without, 179

Execution
as nitty-gritty details, 29–30
for pizza restaurant, 31
Trinity of Creativity as, 26, 31, 34
variations in, 32–33

Exploitive sales
by Columbia House, 161–165
complacency and, 158, 162
costs of, 162
innovation versus, 164–165
reversal of, 163–164

Exploration permission, 85, 139

F

Failure
analytical thinking and, 12
child thinking and, 139
creativity lack for, 168
fear of, 141
humor on, 63
indifference to, 96, 139
inflated ego and, 96
permission for, 63
today and tomorrow, 180

Faucet tap
as ideas flowing, 121–122
self-doubt and, 121–122

Fear
of failure, 141
learning from, 142
types of, 141–143

Ferrari, 171

Fleming, Alexander, 83–84

Focus
analytical thinking and, 81
creativity from, 133
on little victory, xii
multitasking versus, 132

Four Ps for growth, xiii, 105–114

G

Gates, Bill, 13–14

Grant, Ulysses S., 167

Grit, 96, 139
little victory and, 79

Group efforts, 34

Growth
for creativity, 105–106
from Four Ps, xiii, 105–114
by Pan Am Airlines, 165–166
people, process, product, profit for, 106

H

Harmonic theory, 134–135

Henry, Joseph, 84

Herzl, Theodor, 7–8

Hiring, 133, 149
emotional intelligence and, 40
on personal abilities, 107–108

Hitler, Adolf, 170

Human attributes, xii. *See also* People
artificial intelligence without, 43
computers and, 38–39
creativity exercise and, 43–44
creativity for, 49
in emotional intelligence, 44
hiring on, 107–108

Humor, xii, 86
for connections, 64
on control, 63
for creativity, 62
creativity sparked by, 63–64

Humor *(cont'd)*
  on failure, 63
  problems overcome by, 62

I

Ideas
  business needing, 30–31
  as championed, xiii
  change from, 143
  for companies, 3–4
  control killing, 53
  creative idea economy and, xiv,
    16, 173
  exercise for, 29, 52–53
  faucet tap and flowing, 121–122
  grand adjustments in, 33
  large developments from, 47
  for pizza restaurant, 31
  positive thinking for, 55, 122–123
  practical specifics in, 28–29
  RUST against, 145–146
  self-doubt opposite of, 124
  significant variations in, 33–34
  Trinity of Creativity as, 26, 31, 34
Imagination
  children and, 18
  creativity capturing, 48
  on root causes, 52–53
In person meetings, 129–130
Inflated ego. *See* Ego
Innovation
  creation of, xiv
  as creative equity, 153–154
  creativity as, 93
  exploitive sales versus, 164–165
  mistakes breeding, 85
  from Trinity of Creativity, 31–32
Intellectual property, xvii
Internet, 129, 153
  on Toys "R" Us, 160
Inventory problem, 54–55, 63–64
iTunes, 164

J

Jobs, Steve, 11, 13–15, 22
Johnson & Johnson, 148–155
Judgment, 66–67

K

Kodak, 137–138, 140, 143, 145, 158

L

Language of permission, 53
Lazarus, Charles, 159
Leadership
  ever-flexible path by, 97
  inflated ego as ineffective, 96
Life expectancy, 174–175
Listening
  to competition, 66–67
  courage as, 68
  distrust of, 75
  empathy as, 65–66
  external empathy as, 64, 66–67
  microlistening in, 73–74
  modernity and, 75
  skills for, xii
  too much or too little, 71
Little victory, 102–103
  barriers and limitations lifted
    for, 79
  big win versus, 81–82
  creativity from, 81
  disorder and detour in, 79–80
  focus on, xii
  opportunities in, 81
  process as, 109
  success from, 77–78, 95
Love imperfection, 87

M

McDonald's, 80–81
Meetings
  action items from, 72–73
  as in person, 129–130
  purpose for, 72

Mercedes, 169–170
Microlistening, 73–74. *See also*
    Listening
Microsoft, 13–14
Mistake utility
    examples of, 88–89
    stop, love imperfection, rethink
        in, 87
    value seen with, 84–85
Mistakes
    avoidance of, 85
    for better outcome, 88
    break away and recognition on,
        172
    comfort as, 127
    control as, 88, 102
    creativity from, 83–84
    as opportunities, 85
    Post-it Notes from, 88
    responses after, 86
    safety glass from, 88
    Toll House cookie from, 89
    value of, xii
Multitasking, 127–129,
        133–135
    analytical thinking on,
        131–132
    exercise on, 130–132
    focus versus, 132
    limits on, xiii, 130

N
Natural instincts, 102–103
Nazi Party, 170–171
Negative, 53–55
Neuroplasticity
    brains changing as, 5
    old dogs and new tricks in,
        8
New idea. *See* Ideas
Norms questioned, 101–102

O
Opportunities
    in little victory, 81
    mistakes as, 85

P
Pan Am Airlines, 145
    on change, 166–167
    competition for, 166
    complacency by, 166
    with computers, 165
    growth by, 165–166
Paralysis of choice
    complacency and, 158
    creativity not used in, 166
    as stagnation, 167
    time versus, 167–168
Parks, Griffith, 119
Past
    assumptions from, 179
    future from, 172–173
    positive thinking leaving, 57
    recognition of, 173
Penicillin, 83–84
People
    creativity for, 49
    for growth, 106
    hiring and abilities of, 107–108
    human attributes and, 38–39,
        43–44, 107–108
    personality traits of, xii
    process for, 109–110
    stimulation of, 50
    treatment of, 108
Permission
    from consumers, 168
    for exploration, 85, 139
    to fail, 63
    language of, 53
Pizza restaurant, 31
Porsche
    competition for, 171

Porsche *(cont'd)*
  Nazi Party and, 170–171
  reinvention by, 169–171
  sports cars by, 171
Porsche, Ferdinand, 170–171
Porsche, Ferry, 171
Positive thinking
  for actionable plan, 55
  on carbon dioxide emissions, 177
  on charitable giving, 175–176
  on clean drinking water, 176–177
  creativity with, 52–54
  on life expectancy, 174–175
  negative versus, 53–55
  as options and ideas, 55, 122–123
  past left by, 57
  on self-doubt, 122
Post-it Notes, 63
  mistake producing, 88
  shotgun experiment with,
    124–125
Potential, 17–18, 103
  analytical shunning, 118
  Creativity seeing, xvi, 44
  disorder and detour in, 79–80
  variations as, 33–34
Problem solving
  analytical thinking and, x, 51–52
  children and, 18, 21
  courage, humor, empathy for, 62
  creativity for, x, xv, 38–39
  exercise for, 20–21
  on inventory, 54–55, 63–64
  of root problem, 51–53, 55–56
Process
  for communication, 109
  concept, idea, execution in, 26
  consistency for, 110
  with creativity, 109
  for growth, 106
  as little victories, 109
  at personal levels, 109–110

Product
  analytical thinking on, 111
  communication as, 27, 111
  creative definition of, 111–112
  for growth, 106
  identifying, 110
  safety and standards of, 154
  from Trinity of Creativity,
    31–32, 111
Profit
  analytics on, 39, 112–113, 157
  creativity on, 93, 112–114
  for growth, 106
  lack of, 141–142

Q
Quantification, 39

R
Recognition
  of mistakes, 172
  of past, 173
Reinvention
  for creative economy, xiv, 16, 173
  Porsche and, 169–171
Relatability, 150–151
Rest upon success tool (RUST),
  145–146
Restructuring, 12, 15
Results
  actionable plan for, 135
  comfort not for, 102
Rethink outcome, 87–88
Risk
  change as, 22
  creativity and calculated, 15
  as uncomfortable, 133
  yes to, 140
Root problem
  in business, 51–52
  creative options on, 55–56
  imagination on, 52–53

RUST. *See* Rest upon success tool

S

Safety
  mistake for glass and, 88
  product standards for, 154
Salk, Jonas, 48
Sasson, Steve, 137–138
Self. *See also* Ego
  courage and, 68
  creative mind in, 32–33
  creativity as, 100
  ego as, 93
Self-doubt, 143, 179
  action prevented by, 117–118
  in analytical thinking, 120–121,
    125
  from comfort, 119–120
  community and, 125
  control of, 117
  courage and, 68
  creative thinking and, 39
  as disease, xiii, 117
  ego and, 93
  faucet tap and, 121–122
  ideas opposite of, 124
  positive thinking on, 122
  shotgun banishing, 123
  tools against, 121–125
Shotgun
  Post-it Notes and, 124–125
  self-doubt banished with, 123
Shutting up, 74
Sight
  of different ways, xvi, 44
  neuroplasticity for, 5
Solutions
  boundaries pushed for, 85, 139
  by creativity, 93
  creativity for, 32
  from Trinity of Creativity, 31–32
Spread of creativity, 47–48

Stagnation
  at Apple, 12
  movement away from, 173
  paralysis of choice and, 167
Stops, 87
Success
  blame on lack and, 97
  for inflated ego, 94–95
  as little victories, 77–78, 95
  little victory versus, 81–82
  as questioned, 95
  RUST and, 145–146
Switch gears, 133

T

Target, 160
  analytical thinking on, 81
Technology
  from adversity, 45–47
  from Apple, 11–15, 49
  artificial intelligence and, 42
  CCD microchip in, 137
  for comfort, 128
  computers as, 11–15, 38–39,
    42–43, 49, 127–135, 165
  detox day shutting off, 129
  digital camera as, 138
  isolation from, 128
  limits on, xiii
  release from, 128–135
Time, 179
  change as constant and, 11
  character in bad, 99
  as commodity, 75–76
  failure and, 180
  paralysis of choice versus, 167–168
  relevancy and change for, 144
Toll House cookie, 89
Tools
  creativity as, 5–6
  RUST and, 145–146
  against self-doubt, 121–125

Toys "R" Us, 145
  Internet influencing, 160
  Lazarus of, 159
Trinity of Creativity, 23
  as concept, idea, execution, 26,
    31, 34
  group efforts on, 34
  innovation, solutions from,
    31–32
  product captured with, 31–32,
    111
Trust, 148–149
  blame not in, 152
  cost of restoring, 151–155
  Johnson & Johnson on, 151–152
  vulnerability for, 149–151
Tylenol, 147–155

U
Uncomfortable. See also Comfort
  creativity from, 134
  risk with, 133

V
Volkswagen, 170
Vulnerability
  connections from, 150
  control versus, 150
  Johnson & Johnson showing,
    149–151

W
Wakefield, Ruth, 89
Walmart, 160
Westmoreland, Tamarah, 119
"What now" moments, 4
Will power, 7–8
www.nirbashan.com/
  thecreatormindset, 180

Y
Yes, 140

Z
Zika virus, 118–119

About the Author

NIR BASHAN IS A world-renowned creativity expert. He has taught thousands of leaders and individuals around the globe how to harness the power of creativity to improve profitability, increase sales, and ultimately create more meaning in their work.

Nir has spent the past two decades working on a formula to codify creativity. That formula is found in *The Creator Mindset*, which has been translated into two languages. He was one of the youngest professors ever selected to teach graduate courses at the ArtCenter College of Design in Pasadena and also taught undergraduate courses at the University of California at Los Angeles. He has worked on numerous albums, movies, and advertisements with famous actors and musicians ranging from Rod Stewart to Woody Harrelson. His work on creativity has won a Clio Award and was nominated for an Emmy.

Nir is the founder and CEO of The Creator Mindset, a consulting company that does workshops, coaching, and keynote speeches at conferences and corporate events. His clients include AT&T, Microsoft, Ace Hardware, NFL Network, EA Sports, JetBlue, and others.

Nir lives in Orlando, Florida, with his wife, young son, and two Bernedoodles named P-Paws and Waylon Jennings.

A Note on the Type

I T IS IMPORTANT to look at everything through the lens of The Creator Mindset, and typography is no exception. Typography is basically the craft of producing letters, numbers, and symbols. There are probably millions of type sets, but the one chosen for this book is Sabon, a typeface designed by Jan Tschichold in 1967.[1] Tschichold created this typeface just seven years before his death in 1974,[2] and it stands today as one of the world's most beloved type settings. Sabon is characterized by elegance, beautiful serif subtleties, and impactful readability. With Sabon, Tschichold was trying above all to emphasize function.[3]

Today it may seem passé to talk about type, but in 1933 Tschichold's idea of a type that would empathize function was seen as revolutionary. It was perceived as such a grave threat by the Nazi Party that his home and his belongings in Munich were ransacked, he was called a Soviet sympathizer, and he was thrown in jail for six weeks.[4] All this only 10 days after the Nazi Party came to power in Germany. That's how high he was on the Nazi hit list for producing the ideas that led to the typeface you are reading today, the ideas that form these very words and letters.

There were originally three weights Tschichold created for Sabon: normal, *italic*, and **semibold**, all of which are in use in various pages of this book.[5] This typeface has improved the look and feel of this book in immeasurable ways. Tschichold once said:

> **To remain nameless and without specific appreciation, yet to have been of service to a valuable work and to the small number of visually sensitive readers—this, as a rule, is the only compensation for the long, and indeed never-ending, indenture of the typographer.**[6]